KATHRYN POPPER

HONORABLE HIBACHI

A delectable and versatile collection of recipes
inspired by the indoor/outdoor Japanese charcoal grill
and elegantly suitable for every type of broiler and stove

DRAWINGS BY GRAMBS MILLER

SIMON AND SCHUSTER   NEW YORK

SECOND PRINTING

LIBRARY OF CONGRESS CATALOGUE CARD NUMBER: 64-15350
MANUFACTURED IN THE UNITED STATES OF AMERICA
DESIGNED BY EDITH FOWLER

Contents

INTRODUCTION

Introduction

Nobody knows who cooked the first piece of meat over an open fire—or when. The use of fire for cooking food, first to preserve it and later to improve its flavor, is very old.

If food was scarce, primitive man ate furtively and alone and came out of hiding only when his appetite was satisfied. But man is gregarious, and so when food was plentiful he shared it. Also, to cook and share the meat of an animal he had killed was a way of having his neighbors know of his achievement.

Today there may be pride and vanity involved in entertaining, but with advancing civilization, hospitality and generosity are added. Thus, innovations which add warmth or unusual quality to entertaining are welcomed. This contributes to the growing popularity of barbecues and outdoor grills.

The major concern of this book is to introduce the "hibachi" to those of you for whom it may be only a word. Or perhaps you know what it is but are not quite sure what to do with it.

The uses of the hibachi are many, it knows no seasons, and it can make eating a pleasurable ceremony and fun.

Today in America we have the most modern equipment for cooking and preparing food ever known. The hibachi is not intended to replace these advances. But when the palate tires of the camouflaged food of civilization, it can savor food cooked in the time-honored way, any time, and place, by use of the hibachi.

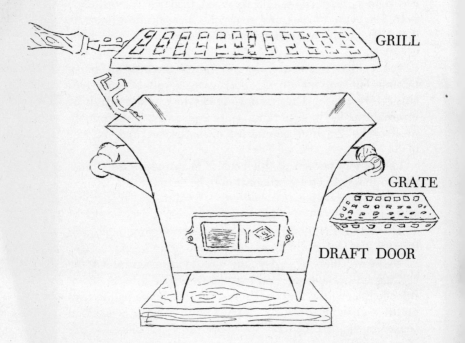

GRILL

GRATE

DRAFT DOOR

The Hibachi – What Is It?

"Hibachi" in Japanese means "fire basin." This portable charcoal burner, probably of Chinese origin, has been in use for centuries in one form or another throughout the Orient, providing heat for the room and the ever present tea pot, serving as a stove for cooking and as a focal point for family gatherings.

In the Far East the hibachi may be made of such exotic materials as mulberry, pagoda or persimmon wood, porcelain or bronze. The traditional Japanese trousseau has always contained at least three hibachis, in addition to lacquered rice buckets, ladles and wooden pillows. A popular form of hibachi in Japan is a round vessel with live charcoals in the center, around which are heaped ashes in the shape of a crater. To the aesthetic Japanese, this is a reminder of the original fires of their beloved Fujiyama.

The hibachi can also be a delightful addition to the American home. It is inexpensive, simple to operate and can be used indoors or out, the year round. With our growing interest in open-fire cooking and our increasing desire to experiment with food from different lands, this type of burner can be most practical.

No matter what the size or shape, the basic parts and principles are the same. The hibachi unit is made (from top to bottom) as follows:

1. Grill, with handles. This is the cooking surface. This grill can be moved to start the fire, to add fuel, to adjust the firebed and for cleaning purposes. Approximately three to four inches below this is:

2. Removable grate for charcoal and firebed. This fits over:

3. Bottom section of unit which holds paper and kindling

to start fire, and which is receptacle for ashes. On this bottom section is:

4. The draft door, a small vent which can be opened and closed to control the intensity of the fire by regulating the flow of air through the unit.

Types of Hibachis

Hibachis range in size from tiny individual burners to large double-grill models twenty-four by twelve inches in size. They come in round, square and rectangular shapes. Although most hibachis are made of black cast-iron (or other metal), there are several novelty models in brightly colored ceramic or heavy porcelain.

Many of the newer model hibachis are equipped with one-hand or touch control for adjusting the grill to three different levels from the coals; some have greaseless grids with pouring wells to reduce smoke and flare-up; some of the models are permanently mounted on individual wooden chopping blocks; and all true hibachis have adjustable drafts.

Prices will vary with the size of the hibachi, but the cost generally ranges from below three dollars to twenty-five. A medium-size hibachi is usually under ten dollars.

Hibachis can be found in the housewares departments of many large department stores, in specialty housewares shops, hardware stores, in some of the bigger supermarkets, and in many Oriental food and novelty shops.

Partial listing of stores which will fill mail orders for hibachis: Miya Co., Inc., 373 Park Avenue South, New York, N.Y.; Eastern Trading Co., Inc., 2801 Broadway, New York, N.Y.; Oriental Food Shop, 1302 Amsterdam Avenue, New York, N.Y.; Takashimaya, Inc., 562 Fifth Avenue, New York, N.Y.

What Size Hibachi?

The answer depends on what you want to use it for.

Even the very small hibachis are fun for hors d'oeuvres. For a successful and amusing cocktail party, provide one of these little burners for each two or three guests. Then let them select and grill their own appetizers.

For other than small kebab-type use, the most manageable size is the ten-inch round (or square) or nine by eleven-inch hibachi, with adjustable grill. These are large enough to be useful, yet small enough to be portable for traveling, picnics, beach, boat or to bring to the table.

If you have a backyard, a terrace, or other more or less permanent spot, the large ten or twelve by twenty-inch hibachi will double your cooking surface and is a worth-while investment.

Whatever size you choose, be sure the hibachi is sturdy and not just a toy.

Charcoal and Lighters

The two main types of charcoal are lump and briquette.

Briquettes cost slightly more than lump charcoal but are preferable for hibachis because they make a more even, consistently hotter and longer lasting fire. Lump charcoal can be used: it lights more quickly and gives a more intense initial heat, but it burns out faster and is more difficult to arrange in an even bed of coals.

There is also a special smokeless charcoal made especially for hibachis but it is much more expensive than regular charcoal and is not readily available.*

Charcoal briquettes are packaged in two to forty-pound bags. They also come in small self-starter cartons which are very good for the small hibachis.

* Takashimaya, Inc., 562 Fifth Avenue, New York, N.Y.

Charcoal can be bought in hardware stores, supermarkets, and wherever fuel is sold.

Lighters: There are several types of electric charcoal lighters and dozens of chemically treated quick starters. Most of these are effective, but for a minimum of flame and smoke, use a foam spray, an electric lighter or the small chemically treated squares resembling compressed sawdust.

Where to Use It

The hibachi can be used outdoors or inside.

For indoor use, if you have a fireplace, by all means utilize the chimney flue to carry off whatever smoke may result when the fire is lit. If you have a terrace, a back stoop, a fire escape or a range hood, start your fire there. However, you can start your hibachi almost anywhere by using an electric lighter or one of the recommended chemically treated quick starters.

How to Start a Fire

1. An hour before you plan to use the hibachi, remove top grill; open draft door at bottom.
2. Arrange a single layer of briquettes on fire grate. Allow space between briquettes so air can circulate. Spray on chemical starter, following instructions. Toss lighted match onto briquettes. Do not use additional starter. (When using an electric charcoal starter or compressed chemically treated starters, arrange briquettes according to manufacturers' directions).
3. In about ten minutes a grayish ash will begin to show. This means the charcoal has begun to burn. With tongs you may occasionally turn briquettes over or move an unburned briquette next to one which has started to burn. This first layer is your pilot fire.

4. When pilot fire is covered with gray ash and a reddish glow begins to show, gently tap off ash with tongs, and add enough additional briquettes to build up a solid base of coals. Close the draft door and have patience. The fire will now take care of itself.

5. When briquettes are reduced to a bed of glowing coals, with no black areas showing, the fire is ready to use. If for any reason you have to delay cooking, add more briquettes to keep up level of coals. If you need additional heat while you are cooking, add briquettes at the edges, and push them toward center when they are well kindled.

6. A simple way to light the hibachi outdoors or in a fireplace: Remove grill and grate. Lightly wad several sheets of newspaper, place in bottom of burner and top with a few small pieces of kindling. Replace charcoal grate. Fill loosely with single layer of charcoal. Open draft door and ignite paper with match. When reddish glow appears, turn briquettes with tongs and add as much charcoal as needed. Close draft.

Never use kerosene or gasoline to start charcoal. It is dangerous and gives food an unpleasant taste.

What to Use Your Hibachi For

Almost anything that can be cooked on a flat outdoor grill can be cooked on a hibachi. The size of your burner will determine the quantity of food and the number of guests you can handle.

Nothing serves better as a conversational ice-breaker than to grill hot appetizers in the living room on the hibachi and serve them piping hot direct from the fire.

If you are using your hibachi for the main course, your

guests will love watching and smelling the process while they have their before-dinner drinks.

In addition to direct charcoal-grilling, the hibachi provides a perfect medium for another type of cooking. Many foreign dishes, particularly in the Oriental cuisines, require very quick cooking, with continuous stirring, in a heavy pot or skillet over intense heat. To be at their best, such "stir-fry" foods must be served immediately. With a high bed of hot coals, the hibachi provides the necessary heat, so what better way than to bring your hibachi right to the table? Half the fun of sukiyaki, for instance, is to see the attractive and colorful array of ingredients, then watch them go into the sizzling pan, a few at a time. Here, too, the aroma of the food as it cooks adds a great deal to the pleasure of eating it.

Or try this: Use your hibachi for the first course and after dinner come back to a pot of coffee and chestnuts which will match those of any street vendor's in the world.

Another use: As we have remarked, the hibachi is excellent for a cocktail party. If you have prepared a variety of kebab-type appetizers in advance, the cocktail party can be turned into an informal and festive supper by adding a green salad, cheese, fruit and coffee.

When you take a family car trip, eating every meal in a restaurant can be very expensive. If you have a hibachi and a bag of charcoal in the car trunk, you can stop occasionally at a roadside stand or market and buy the makings for a home-grilled dinner. If you buy frozen food a few hours before your stopover for the night, it will thaw out en route and be ready when you arrive.

For picnics: Many areas have no outdoor cooking facilities. Others have limited and improperly maintained outdoor grills. There is no problem if you take along your own hibachi.

For boats: You probably are able to manage very well with the galley equipment aboard, but nothing tastes better than charcoal-broiling your own catch or fresh meat or chicken when you drop anchor in port.

What Not to Use Your Hibachi For

Don't try to prepare an entire meal on a single hibachi.
Don't use it for cuts of meat that require long cooking.
Don't use it for meat or for fowl that has a high fat content.
Don't use it for roasts.

Tools

In addition to the hibachi, charcoal and starter, you will need the following basic equipment:
   Kitchen tongs
   Flat spatula
   Basting brush
   Asbestos mitt or heavy pot holder
   Metal or bamboo skewers
   Flat, hinged toaster grill
   Flat, hinged basket grill (optional)
   Heavy skillet (for stir-fry)
   Glove for handling charcoal
   Charcoal scuttle or container (optional)
   Basting tube or sprinkler (for flare-ups)

There are other frills you may want to add, but they are not basic needs.

Tips and Suggestions

1. Cold meat takes longer to cook. Allow it to reach room temperature before grilling. *Exception:* Keep ground meat under refrigeration until ready to grill.
2. Leave seafood and fish in the refrigerator until ready to use, as they taint quickly.
3. Trim excess fat from meat. Flare-up caused by dripping fat will result in smoke and charring. If some flare-up does occur, use the basting tube to squirt just enough water to control the flame without diminishing heat.
4. When marinating, use a glass, pottery or plastic container. Most marinades contain lemon juice, vinegar or wine, which create an acid base, so it is necessary to avoid aluminum pots. Cover the container with a tight lid or aluminum foil, plastic wrap or waxed paper. To achieve uniform penetration, stir marinade at least three or four times.
5. A flat spatula or kitchen tongs should be used to turn meat. A fork will pierce meat, allowing juices to escape.
6. Use a well-oiled, hinged hand-grill or flat basket-grill for small whole fish, fish fillets or other foods which tend to break easily. Instead of turning individual pieces, the whole grill can be flipped over.
7. When using bacon, partially cook to remove excess fat.
8. Before arranging ingredients for hibachi cooking, line a tray or platter with aluminum foil, folding up a small rim around the edge to catch marinade or juices.
9. Skewers: Bamboo skewers in many sizes are available in most Oriental food and novelty shops. They are excellent for small hors d'oeuvres. To prevent the bamboo from burning, soak skewers in water for an hour or more before using. There are many types and sizes of metal skewers on the market. Those of stainless steel with handles or curved ends are the most practical.
10. Set up a table near the hibachi large enough for the

tray of food, utensils, napkins, serving dishes and a container of water.

11. Don't be afraid of seasoning, but too many spices in one dish will cancel each other out. Learn which herbs and spices complement each other.

12. Don't overcook. Food will be tasteless. It is difficult to say exactly how much time is needed for grilling any particular food. Timing depends on so many factors in addition to personal taste: size of hibachi, air flow, intensity of heat, the height of the bed of coals, and the shape, size and quality of the food. Use the suggested time as a gauge, and test food to see if it is properly done.

13. Don't be afraid to experiment and don't be frightened by the number of ingredients in a recipe. If something sounds interesting to you, try it.

14. Clean your grill thoroughly after each use. Soak in water, remove all food particles with steel wool or a stiff brush. A beer can opener is excellent for scraping off burned-on food particles between the bars of the grill. After drying, rub a small amount of oil on the grill.

15. Take ordinary fire-prevention precautions: Don't start fire near curtains; always have a window slightly open when using the hibachi indoors. If there are still burning coals when you are through using the fire, lift them from the grate with tongs and drop them into a bucket of cold water.

16. Don't throw out the ashes. They make fine fertilizer for your house plants or garden.

Special Hints for Stir-Fry Skillet Cooking

1. Since stir-fry cooking requires intense heat, you must have a high, full bed of coals. As the charcoal burns, the level of the firebed will lower.

2. Set the hibachi on a large wooden chopping block or board to prevent damage to table surface or cloth.

3. The Chinese stir-fry in a *wok*, a round metal bowl-shaped pot, but a heavy cast-iron skillet sits more securely on the grate.

4. When the oiled pan is hot, add the first ingredients carefully because of possible spattering.

5. The best tool for stirring and turning is either a stiff spatula or a long-handled wooden spoon. If you are adept, you can use long chopsticks.

6. Store each prepared vegetable in an individual plastic bag and refrigerate until ready to set up your tray.

7. A few recipes require that one of the ingredients be cooked separately and removed temporarily to another dish. In such a case a small electric tray near the hibachi is useful.

8. An egg timer, although not essential, can be helpful.

9. As an additional guide for quick reference you might jot a few notes on a small index card. For example: List ingredients in the order to be used, and cooking time for each.

10. Have a family trial run with one of the recipes. You will be able to check timing, and to get the general feel.

SUGGESTED MENUS

Suggested Menus

1

Pirozhki *(page 188)*

Spicy Chinese Chicken *(page 127)*
Fluffy White Rice *(page 189)*
Artichoke Hearts and Peeled Tomato Quarters
with Vinaigrette Sauce

Chilled Fruit Tray with Litchi Nuts (canned in syrup),
Loquats, Pineapple Spears, Young Stem Ginger
and Mandarin Orange Sections

2

Stuffed Grape leaves

Skewered Lamb, Greek Style *(page 96)*
Special Eggplant Casserole *(page 198)*

Raspberry Sherbet

3

Antipasto Platter

Charcoal-Grilled Tenderloin of Beef *(page 72)*
Baked Potatoes with Assorted Garnishes
(sour cream, chopped chives, grated Parmesan cheese,
chopped fresh dill)
Endive Salad

Avocado Ice Cream *(page 209)*

Vanilla Wafers

4

*An informal menu combining four hot hors d'oeuvres
with a salad and dessert.*

Skewered Beef Strips with Fruit and Rum *(page 48)*
Rumaki *(page 44)*
Grilled Shrimp with Caviar Dip *(page 35)*
Bulgarian Kebabches *(page 51)*

Hot French Bread
Lentil Salad Platter *(page 205)*

Lemon Meringue Pie

5

Eggplant Caviar

Shishkebab *(page 94)*
Very Special Rice *(page 192)*
Sweet and Sour Garden Salad *(page 208)*

Fresh Fruit

Assorted Cheeses

Crackers

6

Fresh Shrimp Cocktail

Grilled Duckling with Honey and Wine *(page 138)*
Orange Rice with Mint *(page 190)*
Tossed Green Salad with Anchovy Dressing *(page 207)*

Ice Cream Puffs with Chocolate Sauce

7

Jellied Consommé Madrilène

Curried Lamb Meatballs with Curry Sauce
(pages 104 and 105)
Fluffy White Rice *(page 189)*
Curry Condiments *(pages 200 to 202)*

Rum-Chestnut Dessert *(page 211)*

8

Chicken Consommé

Unadorned Lamb Chops, Charcoal-Grilled *(page 101)*
Hungarian-Style Noodles *(page 194)*
Avocado-Tomato Mousse Ring *(page 204)*

Apple Pie

9

Raw Vegetable Assortment
with Red Caviar and Sour Cream Dip

Steak Kebabs with Kumquats and Green Peppers *(page 67)*
Savory Wild Rice *(page 193)*

Chocolate Mousse

10

Thin-sliced Hard Salami with Fresh Pumpernickel
Stuffed Hard-Boiled Eggs

Skewered Lamb with Sweetbreads and Tomatoes
(page 100)
Pilaf of Groats and Mushrooms *(page 193)*

Fruit and Cheese

11

Herring in Wine Sauce
Guacamole and Toast Squares

Grilled Chinese Hamburgers *(page 86)*
Three-Bean Salad *(page 204)*
Hot Potato Sticks

Fruit Medley *(page 210)*

12

Chilled Tomato-Clam Juice Cocktail

Flaming Lobster *(page 164)*
Fluffy White Rice with Pignola Nuts
Baked Peppers with Tomatoes and Anchovies *(page 199)*
Hot Herbed French Bread

Fruit Compote and Wafer Cookies

(Serve with well-chilled dry white wine.)

13

Cheese Assortment with Crackers
Radish Roses with Sweet Butter

Skewered Chicken Livers
with Mushroom Caps and Artichoke Hearts *(page 133)*
Baked Curried Chestnuts *(page 200)*

Fresh Berries with Sour Cream

14

Smoked Oysters and Smoked Mussels
with Toasted Rye Squares

Beek Sukiyaki *(page 79)*
Fluffy White Rice *(page 189)*

Chilled Kumquats, Mandarin Orange Segments,
Preserved Ginger and Pineapple Spears

15

Iced Garden-Yoghurt Soup *(page 187)*

Swordfish Steak with Lime and Herbs *(page 158)*
Boiled Fresh Young Vegetables, served on a platter
with lots of butter and chopped fresh parsley
(small new potatoes in jackets, tiny carrots,
little beets, cauliflower and new asparagus)

Chilled Watermelon

16

Celery Stalks with Roquefort Filling
Green and Black Olive Assortment

Grilled Marjoram Chicken *(page 125)*
Savory Brown Rice with Giblets *(page 19)*
Thick Beefsteak-Tomato Slices with Oil and Vinegar

Vanilla Ice Cream with Brandied Peach Halves

17

Steamed Clams

Grilled Butterfish *(page 144)*
Hot Buttered Corn on the Cob
Radish Relish *(page 202)*

Lemon Ice and Assorted Cookies

18

Prosciutto Ham and Avocado Slices

Mexican Burgers *(page 84)*
Baked Chick-Peas *(page 197)*
Indian Garden Salad *(page 208)*

Spiced Nectarines and Nuts with Sour Cream *(page 179)*

19

Stuffed Eggs with Curry
Carrot Sticks, Cherry Tomatoes, Scallions

Grilled Ham Cubes with Bananas, Figs and Port Wine
(page 109)
Lima Bean and Apple Casserole *(page 196)*
Sesame Slaw *(page 206)*

Nuts Roasted in Their Shells *(page 183)*
Cheese Tray and Fresh Fruit

20

Scandinavian Shrimp *(page 35)*

Leg of Baby Lamb with Mushrooms and Pan-Roasted Potatoes
Minted Cucumber Salad with Yoghurt *(page 209)*

Pears with a Touch of Orange *(page 181)*

21

Tiny Cocktail Franks and Martini Onion Kebabs
with Dip *(page 46)*

Ham Cubes with Pineapple *(page 47)*
Oriental Shrimp *(page 33)*
Roquefort-Mushroom Balls *(page 56)*

Green Salad

Cheese Cake

22

Grilled Lamb Strips with Soy Dip *(page 50)*
Skewered Scallops with Sardine Dip *(page 41)*
Tandoori Shrimp *(page 166)*
Salami Rolls with Sweet Gherkins *(page 55)*

Avocado Salad

Cherry Pie and Ice Cream

23

Charcoaled Lobster, Skewered *(page 39)*
Malayan Pork Saté *(page 54)*
Chicken Livers with Anchovies *(page 45)*

Sweet and Sour Garden Salad

Hot Miniature Danish Pastries *(page 184)*

HORS D'OEUVRES

Hors d'Oeuvres

The hibachi is ideal for many kinds of appetizers. The variety and combinations are only as limited as one's imagination.

If you are serving kebab-type hors d'oeuvres, they can be prepared ahead of time or the ingredients can be so arranged that each guest may select and skewer his own creation.

Many of the recipes in this section may be served as a main course.

Skewered Shrimp Variations

There are many ways to prepare grilled shrimp, and they all go well with other hors d'oeuvres.

To prepare shrimp: Shell, devein, wash and dry them well with paper towels. When they are to be skewered, pierce lengthwise, leaving small spaces between. Don't overcook shrimp or they will be tough.

SHRIMP WITH DILL AND BEER

1 *lb. shrimp, cleaned*
1 *8-oz. can of beer*
3 *Tbsps. chopped fresh dill*
  or 1½ *Tbsps. dried dill*
1 *small onion, grated*

½ *clove garlic, pressed*
½ *tsp. salt*
¼ *tsp. black pepper*
4 *Tbsps. melted butter*

Combine all ingredients, except the butter, and marinate overnight in the refrigerator.

Drain, skewer and brush the shrimp with melted butter.

Grill 4 or 5 minutes over hot coals, turning and basting with more butter.

ORIENTAL SHRIMP

1 *lb. shrimp, cleaned*
⅓ *cup soy sauce*
¼ *cup sesame oil*
1 *Tbsp. brown sugar*

1 *Tbsp. finely chopped fresh*
  ginger root
  or ¾ *tsp. powdered ginger*
3 *scallions, including some of*
  green, chopped fine

Combine all the ingredients and marinate 3 to 4 hours in the refrigerator.

Drain the shrimp, reserving the marinade.

Skewer and grill them over a medium bed of coals 5 or 6 minutes, turning, and basting frequently with marinade.

VODKA SHRIMP

1 *lb. shrimp, cleaned*
2 *oz. vodka*
1 *oz. dry vermouth*
2 *Tbsps. lemon juice*
6 *thin slices lemon peel*
1/3 *cup olive oil*

1/2 *tsp. salt*
2 *or 3 dashes Angostura*
   bitters
2 *Tbsps. finely chopped*
   parsley

Combine all the ingredients and marinate overnight in the refrigerator.

Drain the shrimp, reserving the marinade.

Skewer and grill them over a medium bed of hot coals 5 or 6 minutes, turning, and basting frequently with marinade.

SESAME SHRIMP

1 *lb. shrimp, cleaned*
1/2 *cup sesame seeds*
salt

freshly ground black pepper
4 *Tbsps. melted butter*

Toast sesame seeds by placing in a heavy ungreased skillet over low heat and stirring until browned.

Sprinkle shrimp lightly with salt and pepper. Dip in melted butter. Roll in toasted sesame seeds.

Skewer and grill 6 to 8 minutes over a medium bed of coals, turning to brown evenly.

ANCHOVY SHRIMP

1 *lb. shrimp, cleaned*
2 *Tbsps. lemon juice*
1 *Tbsp. rinsed capers*

4 *anchovy fillets*
6 *Tbsps. melted butter*

Blend the lemon juice, capers and anchovies till smooth. Add butter.

Dip the shrimp in this sauce.

Skewer and grill them 6 to 8 minutes over a medium bed of coals, turning to brown evenly.

SCANDINAVIAN SHRIMP

2 *lbs. shrimp, cleaned*
1 *cup cider vinegar*
1 *bay leaf, crumbled*
6 *peppercorns, crushed*
2 *Tbsps. finely chopped fresh dill*
  or 1 Tbsp. dried dill

1 *Tbsp. chopped fresh tarragon*
  or 1 tsp. dried tarragon
1 *tsp. salt*
¼ *cup olive oil*

Combine all the ingredients except the oil in a glass bowl and refrigerate overnight.

Drain the shrimp, thread them on oiled skewers and brush with oil.

Grill over hot coals 4 or 5 minutes, turning to brown evenly, and brushing with more oil.

Serves 8 to 10 as an hors d'oeuvre, 4 as a main course.

GRILLED SHRIMP WITH CAVIAR DIP

1 *lb. shrimp, cleaned*
1 *tsp. salt*
freshly ground black pepper
½ *cup lemon juice*
4 *Tbsps. melted butter*

Dip:
1 *cup sour cream*
4 *oz. jar of red caviar*
1 *small onion, grated*
2 *Tbsps. lemon juice*
⅛ *tsp. cayenne pepper*

Sprinkle shrimp with salt and pepper and add lemon juice. Marinate for 1 hour in a glass bowl.

Combine sour cream with caviar, onion, lemon juice and cayenne and chill.

Drain and skewer shrimp. Brush with melted butter and grill over hot coals 4 or 5 minutes. Turn to brown evenly and brush again with melted butter.

Serve at once with chilled dip.

JUMBO SHRIMPS, GRILLED IN THE SHELL

1 *lb. jumbo shrimp*
1/3 *cup olive oil*
1 *tsp. oregano*
1/2 *tsp. salt*

freshly ground pepper
4 *Tbsps. minced parsley*
lemon quarters

Combine olive oil and oregano and let stand at room temperature for several hours, stirring occasionally.

Wash shrimp thoroughly in cold running water. Drain and dry well. With a sharp pointed knife, split shell down the back, remove vein, and partially split shrimp along the vein line. Spread shrimp open and skewer to keep flat and meat exposed.

Sprinkle with a little salt and pepper and brush generously with the oregano-olive oil mixture.

Grill over hot coals, with meat toward fire, for 3 minutes. Turn, baste meat again with olive oil, and grill 4 or 5 minutes on shell side.

Remove to serving dish. Squeeze lemon over shrimp and sprinkle with minced parsley.

Serve on small plates with small forks and sharp knives. Better still, just use your fingers. In that case don't forget warm, damp finger towels and paper napkins.

GRILLED HOT MUSTARD SHRIMP

1 lb. medium-size shrimp,
  cleaned
3 Tbsps. powdered mustard
½ tsp. salt
1 tsp. sugar

1 tsp. horseradish powder
¾ cup stale beer
3 Tbsps. melted butter
½ cup duck sauce (optional)

Mix mustard, salt, sugar and horseradish together and add enough beer to make a smooth paste. Gradually add rest of beer to make a thin mustard. Let stand for an hour or so, adding more beer or cold water if it becomes too thick.

Dip shrimp in mustard sauce, skewer and brush with melted butter.

Grill over bed of medium coals for 6 to 8 minutes, turning to brown evenly.

These are *hot*. If possible, serve with a bowl of Chinese duck sauce (available in Chinese restaurants or Oriental grocery stores).

SESAME SHRIMP WITH DILL

2 lbs. medium-size shrimp
1 cup olive oil
½ cup plain yoghurt
2 Tbsps. finely chopped fresh
  dill

1 tsp. salt
½ tsp. freshly ground black
  pepper
¼ cup sesame seeds

Combine olive oil with yoghurt. Add dill, salt and pepper. Pour this over the shrimp. Refrigerate, stirring from time to time, for at least 3 hours.

Remove shrimp from marinade, and roll each one in sesame seeds. Thread on oiled skewers.

Broil over medium hot coals 5 or 6 minutes.

SKEWERED CLAMS WITH BACON

2 doz. whole clams, prefer-
　ably freshly shucked
12 slices lean bacon, partially
　cooked

2 Tbsps. lemon juice
pepper

Partially cook bacon by pan-frying for 3 minutes to render out some of the fat. Do not allow it to become crisp. Cut bacon slices in half.

Remove any shell particles from clams. Sprinkle with lemon juice and a generous twist from the pepper mill.

Wrap each clam in a half-slice of bacon and secure with a well-soaked bamboo or slender metal skewer.

Grill 3 or 4 minutes over medium hot coals, turning to crisp bacon evenly.

COAL-ROASTED CLAMS

2 doz. whole clams, prefer-
　ably freshly shucked
6 Tbsps. butter
2 tsps. anchovy paste

1 tsp. grated lemon rind
3 Tbsp. lemon juice
½ tsp. paprika

Soften butter at room temperature and cream with anchovy paste. Add grated lemon rind.

Make 8 packets of 2 layers of heavy duty foil (each approximately 6 x 8 inches). Spread a little anchovy butter in the center of each packet and on it lay 3 clams in a row. Sprinkle with lemon juice, a little paprika, and add a generous dab of anchovy butter on top of each clam. Seal the packet securely.

Remove the grill from the hibachi. Place the packets directly on the bed of hot coals. Roast for 4 or 5 minutes, turning once with tongs, being careful not to puncture the foil.

Remove to small serving plates and serve in foil.

CHARCOALED LOBSTER, SKEWERED

1½ lbs. uncooked lobster
  meat
  (use either large lobster
tails, completely thawed,
or remove meat from claws
and tails of freshly killed
lobsters)

3 Tbsps. lime juice
1 tsp. salt
¼ lb. melted butter
1 Tbsp. chopped chives
1 Tbsp. chopped parsley

If you use frozen lobster tails, thaw completely, cut down middle of soft under-part of tail and remove meat. Cut into 1-inch pieces. Sprinkle with lime juice and salt and dip into butter combined with chives and parsley. Skewer.

Grill over hot coals, brushing several times with melted butter, and turning to brown evenly. Grill about 6 or 7 minutes in all.

Remove from grill and serve with the remaining butter sauce.

GRILLED OYSTERS WITH BACON JACKETS
(Angels on Horseback)

2 doz. oysters, shucked
¼ tsp. salt
⅛ tsp. black pepper

2 Tbsps. lemon juice
finely chopped parsley
12 thin slices lean bacon

Drain and carefully remove any shell particles from oysters. Season with salt and pepper; sprinkle with lemon juice and finely chopped parsley.

Cook bacon strips for 3 minutes to remove some of the fat (but do not make them crisp). Cut in half.

Wrap each oyster in a half-slice of bacon and thread on a presoaked bamboo or thin metal skewer to secure bacon strip.

Grill over hot coals for 3 minutes, turning to crisp bacon evenly. Do not overcook or the oysters will toughen.

LOBSTER-SHRIMP SURPRISE PACKAGES

1 *large frozen lobster tail*	2 *Tbsps. chopped chives*
12 *medium-size shrimp,*	¼ *cup chopped green olives*
cleaned	2 *Tbsps. sour cream*
4 *oz. cream cheese*	½ *tsp. paprika*
3 *oz. bleu cheese*	4 *Tbsps. dry vermouth*

Thaw the lobster tail, slit soft undershell and remove meat. Cut crosswise into thin slices.

Split the cleaned shrimp in half lengthwise.

Soften the cream and bleu cheese at room temperature. Blend into a smooth mixture with the chives, olives and sour cream.

Using double-duty aluminum foil, cut 8 pieces, 9 inches square. Use 2 thicknesses for each packet. Spread a quarter of the cheese mixture in the center of each packet. Using a quarter of the lobster and 6 shrimp halves for each portion, press them into the cheese mixture. Sprinkle with paprika. Turn up the edges of the foil and pour a tablespoon of vermouth into each. Seal the packet tight.

Grill over medium coals for 10 minutes on each side, turning carefully to avoid puncturing the foil.

Serve in foil, with forks, on individual plates. Use hot French bread to mop up the sauce.

Serves 4.

GRILLED OYSTERS IN THE HALF SHELL

2 *doz. oysters with oyster*	1 *tsp. Worcestershire sauce*
liquid	1-2 *drops Tabasco sauce*
1 *Tbsp. parsley*	2 *Tbsps. dry vermouth*
1 *tsp. chopped tarragon*	6 *Tbsps. butter*
or ¼ *tsp. dry tarragon*	½ *tsp. paprika*
2 *Tbsps. chopped chives*	*lemon wedges*

Open oysters, reserving liquor and curved part of shell.

Strain liquor into blender bowl. Add parsley, tarragon, chives, Worcestershire sauce and Tabasco. Blend until puréed. Add vermouth.

Soften butter at room temperature and blend in puréed herbs and vermouth to make a smooth paste.

Carefully remove any pieces of shell from oysters. Rinse and dry shells. Place 1 teaspoon of the seasoned butter in bottom of each shell, place the oyster on top of the butter and top the oyster with another teaspoon of herb butter. Sprinkle with paprika.

Place the oysters, shell side down, over a high bed of glowing coals. Grill no more than 3 or 4 minutes, or until edges of oysters curl.

Remove oysters (with tongs) to plates and serve hot with lemon wedges.

SKEWERED SCALLOPS WITH SARDINE DIP

1 *lb. scallops*
  (*use bay scallops whole;*
  split sea scallops in half,
  across the grain)
2 *Tbsps. lemon juice*
½ *tsp. salt*
½ *tsp. paprika*
3 *Tbsps. olive oil*

Sardine Dip:
1 *small can boneless sardines*
1 *tsp. capers*
1 *Tbsp. grated orange rind*
2-3 *dashes Angostura bitters*
1 *Tbsp. lemon juice*
¼ *cup mayonnaise*
¼ *cup sour cream*

For dip, drain oil from sardines and mash them to a smooth paste. Add rest of dip ingredients, stir until smooth and chill.

Rinse scallops and pat dry with paper towels. Sprinkle with lemon juice, salt and paprika. Dip in olive oil. Skewer, leaving small spaces between scallops.

Grill over hot coals, turning to brown evenly, for 5 or 6 minutes.

Serve with chilled dipping sauce.

GRILLED SESAME SCALLOPS

1 lb. scallops
(use bay scallops whole;
split sea scallops in half,
across the grain)
1 cup dry white wine or
vermouth

1 tsp. crushed fennel seeds
½ cup sesame seeds, toasted
4 Tbsps. melted butter
½ tsp. salt
¼ tsp. pepper

Rinse scallops and pat dry with paper towels. Cover with wine and crushed fennel seeds in a non-metal container and marinate for several hours.

Toast sesame seeds in a heavy ungreased skillet, stirring until they are browned.

Remove scallops from marinade and drain. Dip them first in melted butter, seasoned with salt and pepper, and then roll in toasted sesame seeds. Skewer, leaving small spaces between.

Grill over hot coals, turning to brown, for 5 or 6 minutes.

SEAFOOD COCKTAIL BALLS WITH SWEET AND SOUR SAUCE
(SKILLET)

¾ lb. medium-size shrimp
¾ lb. flounder fillet
2 Tbsps. peanut oil
½ cup peanuts, ground
½ cup finely chopped onions
2 Tbsps. butter
½ tsp. black pepper
½ tsp. powdered saffron
(optional)
1 Tbsp. cornstarch
1 Tbsp. soy sauce
1 egg, slightly beaten

Sweet and Sour Sauce:
3 scallions, finely sliced
½ cup shredded carrots
½ cup chopped green pepper
2 Tbsps. peanut oil
1 Tbsp. minced fresh ginger
or ¾ tsp. powdered ginger
½ tsp. black pepper
1 cup beef consommé
2 Tbsps. cornstarch
½ cup cider vinegar
2 Tbsps. soy sauce
¼ cup brown sugar

Sweet and sour sauce can be made well in advance, then reheated just before serving. Sauté scallions, carrots and green pepper in peanut oil for 5 minutes. Add ginger, black pepper and consommé. Simmer gently for 10 minutes. Make a thin smooth paste of cornstarch with some of the vinegar, and when well mixed, add balance of vinegar and soy sauce. Add to skillet with brown sugar, stirring constantly until thickened (about 5 minutes). Correct seasoning. If too thick, add additional consommé.

Shell, devein and wash shrimp. Drain and cut into small pieces. Wipe flounder with damp cloth and cut into chunks. Pour 2 tablespoons peanut oil in blender bowl and add pieces of fish and shrimp, not too many at a time. Blend at high speed until smooth. Scrape out blender bowl and repeat, adding peanuts with the fish, until all are blended.

Sauté onions in butter until soft. Remove from heat and season with pepper and saffron. Add onions to blended seafood and nuts. Blend cornstarch with soy sauce and a little cold water, beat with egg, and work into seafood mixture until smooth. Oil palms of hands lightly and form mixture into cocktail-size balls. Cover and refrigerate until ½ hour before ready to cook.

In heavy skillet over high, hot bed of glowing coals, heat 3 tablespoons peanut oil. When hot, add cocktail balls (don't crowd pan), turning to brown evenly. As each batch is done, remove to platter covered with paper towels or brown paper to drain. When cocktail balls are all cooked, pour sweet and sour sauce into skillet, let heat thoroughly and return cocktail balls to pan. Serve in individual dishes or let guests spear from the pot.

CURRIED FISH AND BANANA KEBABS

4 small thin fish fillets
salt
5 Tbsps. melted butter
2 Tbsps. lemon juice

2 Tbsps. chutney
8 1-inch slices of firm ripe
    banana
1 tsp. Indian curry powder

Cut small fillets in half lengthwise. Wipe with damp cloth; sprinkle lightly with salt.

Combine 2 tablespoons melted butter with lemon juice and chutney. Spread in a thin layer on one side of fillets. Dip banana slices into remaining mixture, lay on spread side of fillet and roll up. Secure with a presoaked bamboo skewer.

Combine remaining 3 tablespoons melted butter with curry powder and brush on outside of roll.

Grill over medium low coals for 5 or 6 minutes, turning carefully to brown evenly, and brushing frequently with curry butter.

RUMAKI
(Chicken Livers with Water Chestnuts and Scallions)

6 chicken livers (about ½
    lb.), each cut into 3
    pieces
6 canned water chestnuts,
    drained, each cut into
    3 pieces
9 slices bacon, cut in half
    lengths and partially
    cooked
6 scallions, cut in 1-inch
    pieces

Marinade:
¼ cup soy sauce
¼ cup dry sherry
1 tsp. brown sugar
2 Tbsps. sesame oil
    (optional)
1 slice fresh ginger root,
    1 inch in diameter,
    ¼ inch thick
or ½ tsp. powdered ginger

Combine soy sauce, sherry, brown sugar and sesame oil in non-metallic container. Squeeze in fresh ginger root with garlic press.

With small sharp-pointed knife cut small incision in each piece of chicken liver and insert small piece of water chestnut. Place prepared chicken livers, precooked bacon slices and scallion strips into marinade. Mix well to coat and let stand for at least 1 hour, longer if possible. Drain, reserving marinade.

Wrap a bacon strip around each piece of chicken liver with water chestnut. Secure firmly with small well-soaked bamboo skewer. On 9-inch bamboo skewers place 3 wrapped chicken livers, alternating with scallion slices. Lay on platter and pour reserved marinade over all.

Place on oiled grill over medium hot coals for 5 or 6 minutes, turning to crisp bacon evenly. Serve each skewer on individual plate with small fork. These should be served *hot!*

CHICKEN LIVERS WITH ANCHOVIES

½ lb. chicken livers
½ tsp. MSG or Accent
½ tsp. black pepper

1 2-oz. can flat anchovy
    fillets
3 Tbsps. olive oil

Rinse, dry and halve chicken livers. Sprinkle with MSG and black pepper. Let stand for 15 minutes.

Wrap an anchovy fillet around each chicken liver half and secure with a presoaked bamboo skewer. Brush with olive oil.

Grill over medium hot coals for 5 or 6 minutes, turning to brown evenly, and basting with olive oil.

Shelf Kebabs

There are a number of domestic and imported canned specialty items on the market these days from which you can make quick and tasty kebabs.

Use very thin 6- to 8-inch metal skewers or, preferably, bamboo skewers which have been soaked in water for several hours.

Here are a few suggested combinations:

COCKTAIL MEATBALLS AND GREEN TOMATOES

Drain a can of Danish cocktail meatballs packed in brine. Dip in chili sauce and skewer alternately with tiny green cocktail tomatoes. Grill quickly over medium hot coals, turning to brown evenly. Serve with chili sauce as a dip.

MINIATURE HOLLAND SALAMI AND DILL PICKLE CHIPS

Drain miniature salamis, brush with your favorite prepared mustard, and skewer alternately with pickle chips. Grill for 4 or 5 minutes, over medium coals, turning to brown evenly and heat through. Serve with small bowl of mustard.

TINY COCKTAIL FRANKS AND MARTINI ONIONS, WITH DIP

Combine ½ cup chili sauce, 1 tablespoon Worcestershire sauce, 3 or 4 drops Tabasco sauce, ½ teaspoon onion salt and a little black pepper. Chill. Just before grilling, dip the tiny franks in the sauce and skewer alternately with cocktail onions. Grill 4 or 5 minutes over medium coals. Serve with chilled dip.

VIENNA SAUSAGES WITH HOT MUSTARD

Let this mustard age for at least an hour before using. Combine 4 tablespoons powdered mustard with enough beer to make a thin paste. Stir in 1 tablespoon brown sugar and 1 tablespoon grated horseradish. If it becomes too thick, thin with additional beer. This is very *hot*, and you may prefer to mix it half and half with regular mustard. Drain Vienna sausages, skewer with small spaces between, and grill 4 or 5 minutes over medium coals. Serve with hot mustard.

HAM CUBES WITH SMALL PICKLED BEETS

Cut a small canned ham (or part of it) into ¾-inch cubes. Brush with melted butter seasoned with a little prepared mustard. Skewer alternately with small pickled beets. Grill over medium coals, turning to brown evenly, for 5 or 6 minutes.

HAM CUBES WITH PINEAPPLE

Cut a small canned ham (or part of it) into ¾-inch cubes. Drain a small can of pineapple chunks. Combine the pineapple juice with 2 tablespoons honey, pour over ham cubes and pineapple chunks, and let stand for half an hour. Drain, skewer alternately, brush with melted butter and sprinkle with a little paprika. Grill over medium coals, turning to brown, for 4 or 5 minutes.

SWEDISH FISH BALLS WITH HORSERADISH SAUCE

Combine 1 cup sour cream with 3 tablespoons prepared horseradish and 2 tablespoons chili sauce. Skewer fish balls, brush with melted butter, and grill over medium coals, for 3 or 4 minutes, turning to brown evenly. Serve with chilled horse-radish sauce as dip.

SKEWERED BEEF STRIPS WITH FRUIT AND RUM

1½ lbs. lean tender beef, 1 inch thick, boned
3 Tbsps. guava jelly
½ cup orange juice
2 Tbsps. lime juice

1 Tbsp. grated lime rind
½ tsp. salt
½ tsp. powdered ginger
¼ cup light rum
6 Tbsps. melted butter

Melt guava jelly and combine with orange juice, lime juice, lime rind, salt, ginger and rum.

Trim beef and freeze partially to make slicing easier. Cut across the grain into very thin strips. Thread lengthwise, weaving in S-shape, on well-soaked bamboo skewers.

Lay skewered beef strips in a pyrex or porcelain dish and marinate in rum mixture for several hours. Drain and brush with melted butter.

Grill over hot coals very quickly, no more than ½ minute on each side.

Serve immediately. This is good with thin slices of warm fresh French bread.

BEEF-OLIVE BALLS, SKEWERED

1 lb. lean beef, ground twice
½ tsp. chili powder
½ tsp. salt
2 Tbsps. chili sauce

1 Tbsp. Worcestershire sauce
1 egg yolk, slightly beaten
1 small jar stuffed green cocktail olives, drained

Mix chili powder and salt with chili and Worcestershire sauces. Add, with egg yolk, to ground beef and mix thoroughly.

Shape small portion of meat into bite-size meatball around an olive, completely hiding olive in center. Thread 4 or 5 of these meatballs on a thin skewer (if possible, pierce olive sideways). Chill.

Grill 4 or 5 minutes over hot coals, turning to brown evenly.

Remove skewers to serving dish, remove meatballs from skewers and serve hot with individual cocktail picks.

COCKTAIL MEATBALLS WITH CARAWAY SEEDS
(SKILLET)

1 ½ lbs. lean beef, ground twice
½ cup minced onion
½ cup mushrooms, diced fine
4 Tbsps. butter
2 Tbsps. caraway seeds
2 Tbsps. finely chopped fresh dill
 or 1 Tbsp. dried dill weed
1 tsp. salt
½ cup rye bread crumbs
½ cup stale beer
½ cup sour cream
2 eggs, slightly beaten
2 Tbsps. olive oil

Sauté onion and mushrooms in 2 tablespoons butter until soft. Remove from fire and stir in caraway seeds, dill and salt.

Soak bread crumbs in beer. Squeeze out excess moisture. Combine with ground beef. Add sour cream and onion-mushroom mixture. Mix thoroughly, adding beaten eggs. Chill mixture in covered bowl for 1 hour.

With slightly oiled hands, form mixture into tiny meatballs.

Over high hot bed of coals heat in heavy skillet 2 tablespoons olive oil and 2 tablespoons butter. Lay meatballs in skillet; do not crowd. Brown quickly on both sides and remove with slotted spoon to platter lined with paper towels. Spear with cocktail picks.

These can be served with a hot chili sauce dip.

GRILLED LAMB STRIPS WITH SOY DIP

1½ lbs. baby lamb, in one
    piece from leg
1 cup soy sauce
½ cup dry sherry
¼ cup wine vinegar

1 tsp. sugar
¼ tsp. cayenne pepper
½ cup finely chopped
    scallions

Trim fat and fell from lamb and freeze partially to make slicing easier. With a very sharp knife cut thin strips of lamb, slicing across the grain. Thaw completely and thread lengthwise in S-shape on presoaked bamboo skewers. Lay on a platter.

Combine soy, sherry, vinegar, sugar, cayenne and scallions. Pour half of this sauce over the lamb strips. Turn the skewers to coat meat evenly. Pour the remaining sauce into a dunking bowl.

Grill the lamb strips very quickly over hot coals not much more than a minute, turning to brown both sides. Serve hot and let guests dip them in the sauce.

Have some warm, damp finger towels available.

ARMENIAN COCKTAIL MEATBALLS
(SKILLET)

1 lb. lean lamb, ground twice
3 Tbsps. dried currants
1 onion, chopped
3 Tbsps. olive oil
¼ cup coarsely chopped
    pignolia nuts
1 Tbsp. lemon juice
½ cup cooked white rice

1 Tbsp. fresh mint, chopped
    or 1 tsp. dried mint
¼ tsp. powdered saffron
1 tsp. salt
½ tsp. black pepper
1 egg yolk, slightly beaten
½ cup plain yoghurt
2 Tbsps. butter
lemon

Pour boiling water over currants to soften. Let stand for 10 minutes, drain and chop.

Sauté chopped onion in 1 tablespoon olive oil until tender. Cool, and combine with pignolia nuts, currants, lemon juice, cooked rice, mint, saffron, salt and pepper. Mix lightly with ground lamb, stiring in egg yolk and yoghurt. Chill in covered bowl for 1 hour.

With slightly oiled hands, form mixture into tiny meatballs.

Over high hot bed of coals, heat 2 tablespoons olive oil and 2 tablespoons butter in heavy skillet. Add meatballs (do not crowd). Brown quickly on both sides and remove with slotted spoon to platter lined with paper towels. Spear with cocktail picks and serve hot sprinkled with a little lemon juice.

BULGARIAN KEBABCHES

1 *lb. ground veal*
1 *lb. ground lamb*
1 *medium-size onion,*
    chopped fine
1 *tsp. cumin*

½ *tsp. powdered saffron*
2 *tsps. salt*
1 *tsp. freshly ground pepper*
2 *egg yolks*
¼ *cup ice water*

Thoroughly mix onion, cumin, saffron, salt and pepper into ground veal and lamb. Allow to season for 3 or 4 hours in refrigerator.

Add slightly beaten egg yolks to mixture and blend. Then work the mixture with your hands, adding ice water, a little at a time, until mixture is soft and elastic. Apply olive oil to hands and shape meat into form of fat link sausages, approximately 1 inch thick and 2 inches long. Thread kebabches onto oiled skewers.

Broil over medium hot coals, turning constantly, for 7-8 minutes, or until well browned.

SKEWERED VEAL, MOZZARELLA AND PROSCIUTTO ROLLS

1 *lb. veal scallops, cut thin*
12 *thin slices prosciutto or*
   boiled ham
¼ *lb. mozzarella cheese*
¼ *cup olive oil*

3 *Tbsps. lemon juice*
½ *tsp. oregano*
½ *tsp. salt*
½ *tsp. black pepper*

Pound veal scallops between 2 pieces of heavy waxed paper until very thin. Cut meat into 3-inch widths. Cut ham in slightly smaller pieces and cut cheese into thin strips.

Combine olive oil, lemon juice, oregano, salt and pepper. Pour over veal strips and let stand for 15 minutes.

To make roll: Lay veal strip on sheet of waxed paper, a piece of ham on top of veal, and cheese on ham. Roll up veal, tucking in edges to enclose cheese and secure with a pre-soaked bamboo or thin metal skewer. Brush rolls with olive oil mixture.

Grill 5 or 6 minutes over medium coals, basting with oil, and turning to brown evenly.

Serve on small individual plates. Don't forget paper napkins.

HAM AND CHEESE ROLLS

6 *thin slices boiled ham*
1 *Tbsp. prepared mustard*
4 *thin slices Muenster cheese*

12 *tiny green Italian peppers*
   (canned)

Spread 1 side of ham slices with mustard. Cut each slice of ham in half. Cut Muenster cheese slices into thirds.

Lay 1 slice of cheese on mustard side of ham. Top with small drained pepper. Fold 2 sides of ham over cheese and pepper and secure with an 8-inch bamboo skewer.

Grill over low coals for 3 or 4 minutes on each side.

CHARCOALED COCKTAIL SPARERIBS
(With Sauce and a Caution)

First, the caution: Spareribs are pork, and pork must be well done. However, there is nothing more tasty than spareribs over charcoal. So, for your protection and your pleasure try this. It takes time, but it's worth the effort.

4 *lbs. lean young pork spareribs, sawed in half horizontally and cut into 2-rib serving portions*
1 *large onion, sliced*
1 *Tbsp. caraway seeds*
2 *cups apple cider*
1 *cup sauerkraut juice*

Marinade and Glaze:
4 *Tbsps. vegetable oil*
2 *cups finely chopped sweet onions*
½ *cup finely chopped green pepper*
1 *clove garlic, pressed*
salt and pepper
1 *tsp. crushed red pepper*
1 *cup beef consommé*
¼ *cup vinegar*
¼ *cup brown sugar*

Put spareribs in a deep kettle. Add sliced onion and caraway seeds and cover with cider and sauerkraut juice. Bring to a boil and simmer, covered, over low fire for 1 hour.

While ribs are simmering, make marinade: In a heavy skillet heat vegetable oil and sauté onions, green pepper and garlic. Season with a little salt, pepper and crushed red pepper. Stir in consommé, vinegar and brown sugar and let simmer slowly for 30 minutes, stirring to prevent sticking.

Remove ribs from cider mixture and drain. Place in a non-metal container and cover with marinade, turning to coat thoroughly. Let stand for several hours.

Grill on hibachi, over medium hot coals, for 10 minutes, turning often and basting as necessary, to crisp and brown ribs.

Serve with remaining heated marinade as dip, with plenty of paper napkins or hot damp finger towels.

This will serve 8 to 10 as an appetizer, 4 as main course.

MALAYAN PORK SATÉ

2 lbs. very lean pork
3 cloves garlic
½ cup soy sauce
1 Tbsp. crushed hot pepper

2 Tbsps. dark molasses
3 lemons
1 tsp. salt

Press 1 clove of garlic into soy sauce. Add crushed pepper and dark molasses. Reserve half of this hot sauce for dip. Combine remaining half with lemon juice, 2 pressed garlic cloves and salt. This is for marinade.

Cut meat into small ½-inch pieces, combine with marinade and let stand for 4 hours, turning meat occasionally for even seasoning.

Drain meat and skewer, allowing space between the pieces of meat for thorough browning. Broil over medium coals for at least 20 minutes, turning and basting.

Use reserved hot sauce as dip.

GRILLED SAUSAGES WITH APPLES

1 lb. tiny link pork sausages
1 cup dry white wine
2 Tbsps. butter
3 Tbsps. honey

1 Tbsp. water
1 Tbsp. lemon juice
1 tsp. cinnamon
2 crisp apples

Simmer pork sausages for 20 minutes in white wine. Drain and pat dry with paper towels.

Melt butter, add honey, water, lemon juice and cinnamon. Heat until honey is dissolved. Core and cut unpeeled apples into sixths, lengthwise. Dip pieces immediately in heated honey butter.

Thread sausages and honeyed apple slices alternately on thin skewers. Grill 6 or 7 minutes over medium coals, turning to brown evenly.

SALAMI ROLLS WITH SWEET GHERKINS

16 *tiny slices salami* (*hard Italian or Hungarian type is best*)
16 *tiny sweet gherkin pickles*

Trim casing from outer edges of salami. Wrap a salami slice around a drained pickle. Secure with presoaked bamboo skewer or thin metal skewer.

Grill over hot coals for 2 or 3 minutes, turning. Serve hot.

Appetizers with Bacon Jackets

Bacon enhances the flavor of many grilled hors d'oeuvres, but in order to avoid flame-ups from the dripping fat, parboil the bacon for 5 minutes or partially cook it in a skillet or the oven ahead of time.

MUSSELS

Scrub mussels thoroughly with stiff brush to remove dirt, sand and beard. With a little water, steam in tightly closed kettle until shells open (about 10 minutes). Remove from shells, discarding any mussel which does not open. Wrap each mussel in a half-strip of bacon, and thread, 3 or 4 to a skewer. Grill over medium charcoal until bacon is crisp.

BRAZIL NUTS

Sauté 12 large shelled Brazil nuts in 2 tablespoons melted butter. Salt and drain on paper towel. Wrap each nut in half-slice of bacon. Skewer and grill over medium charcoal until bacon is crisp.

ALMOND-STUFFED OLIVE AND BACON KEBABS

16 *large green olives, stuffed with almonds*
8 *strips lean bacon*

Cook bacon for 3 minutes. Do not crisp. Drain fat. Cut each slice in half.

Wrap each stuffed green olive in a half-slice of bacon. Secure with a presoaked bamboo skewer.

Grill over medium coals until bacon is crisp—3 or 4 minutes at most, turning to brown evenly.

ROQUEFORT MUSHROOM BALLS

1 *lb. mushrooms, approximately 1 inch across (as uniform in size as possible)*
6 *Tbsps. butter*
½ *tsp. salt*

Filling:
3 *oz. Roquefort cheese*
1 *Tbsp. cream*
1 *Tbsp. ground almonds*
1½ *Tbsps. finely grated onion*
½ *tsp. paprika*

Remove stems from mushrooms, clean (peeling if necessary). With a small spoon, scrape the black gills out of the mushroom cap. Heat butter in skillet and gently sauté mushrooms for a few minutes. Salt lightly. Remove from fire.

Allow the cheese to soften at room temperature. Cream it until very smooth, adding cream, nuts, onion and paprika. Fill mushroom caps just level with the edge. Press 2 caps, fitting sides together. It will resemble a small ball. Skewer carefully with a thin skewer, leaving a quarter of an inch between the balls. Brush with butter.

Broil on well-oiled grill over medium hot coals for no more than 3 or 4 minutes, turning to brown evenly.

Serve on small dishes with cocktail picks—and napkins.

PUNGENT LIVER KEBABS

1 *lb. calves' liver*
4 *canned whole roasted*
  pimientos
24 *cocktail onions*
½ *cup lime (or lemon) juice*

2 *Tbsps. grated onion*
½ *tsp. salt*
½ *tsp. turmeric*
½ *tsp. chili powder*
¼ *tsp. cumin powder*
4 *Tbsps. melted butter*

Trim outer skin and veins from liver. Wipe with damp cloth and cut into ¾-inch cubes. Cut pimientos into small squares. Drain cocktail onions.

Thoroughly mix lime juice with grated onion and seasoning. Pour over liver cubes and let stand for a half hour. Drain.

Alternately skewer liver cubes, pimiento squares and cocktail onions. Brush with melted butter.

Grill over medium hot coals for 5 or 6 minutes, basting with butter and turning to brown evenly.

TOASTED HAZELNUTS
(SKILLET)

1 *lb. shelled hazelnuts*
¼ *cup butter*
¼ *cup peanut oil*

½ *tsp. salt*
½ *tsp. onion salt*
1 *tsp. paprika*

In a heavy skillet, over hot bed of coals, heat butter and oil. Add shelled hazelnuts and sauté, stirring with wooden spoon until nuts are golden brown.

Remove pan from heat, sprinkle nuts with salt, onion salt and paprika, and continue stirring for several more minutes until nuts stop browning.

These are delicious served as an hors d'oeuvres with dry sherry or cocktails.

DATES AND CAMEMBERT

24 pitted dates   1 oz. Camembert cheese

Force a small piece of Camembert inside each date. Press closed. Skewer.

Grill over low coals for 4 or 5 minutes, turning.

This is an excellent addition to a tray of hors d'oeuvres.

CURRIED ALMONDS
(SKILLET)

1 cup blanched almonds   1 tsp. curry powder
2 Tbsps. peanut oil   ¼ tsp. garlic salt
2 Tbsps. butter   salt

In heavy skillet, over high bed of hot coals, heat oil and butter. Stir in curry powder and garlic salt.

Add cup of blanched almonds and stir with wooden spoon for 4 or 5 minutes to toast. Remove pan from heat and continue stirring for another minute.

Remove to serving bowl and sprinkle lightly with salt. Serve hot.

GARLIC POPCORN

special corn for popping   ½ clove garlic, pressed
1 cup melted butter   salt

Line bottom of long-handled popcorn popper with foil. Spread thin layer of popping corn over foil, close popper and shake over hot coals until corn is popped. Shake constantly to prevent scorching kernels.

Empty popper into deep bowl. Repeat until you've popped enough corn to start with. Stir in butter to which you have added garlic, and salt to taste, mix through and serve.

VEGETABLES AND FRUITS

Vegetables and Fruits

Grilled Vegetables

On Grilling Vegetables: In many instances, the grilling time for vegetables and meat differs. Some vegetables require less intense heat, and some must be precooked and then grilled to heat and brown. If your hibachi is small, there is also a question of space. In such cases, it is sometimes preferable to skewer vegetables separately, brushing with oil, butter, or the marinade or glaze from accompanying meat. Place the skewers around the edges of the grill. They can be moved to the center for a minute or two, if necessary, after the meat is finished.

NEW POTATOES

Parboil very small new potatoes until tender, but not mushy. Sprinkle lightly with salt. Dip in melted butter and roll in finely chopped fresh dill. Skewer with thin metal skewer and grill, turning, 4 or 5 minutes over medium coals.

ZUCCHINI

Scrub squash, trim the ends, cut into 1-inch slices and simmer for 3 or 4 minutes in a little water. Drain well and season lightly with salt. Prepare a mixture of oregano and olive oil, in the proportion of 1 teaspoon oregano to ½ cup oil, and let stand about 1 hour. Dip the slices of zucchini in this. Skewer sideways, going through the green skin edges, on thin skewers. Grill 5 or 6 minutes over medium coals, brushing with oil and turning to brown both sides.

BABY CARROTS

If you can't find very small new carrots, use the canned variety. Combine 1 teaspoon finely minced fresh mint with ¼ cup melted butter. Dip carrots in mint butter, skewer, and grill 2 or 3 minutes over medium heat, turning to brown, and brushing with a little of the butter.

BRUSSELS SPROUTS

Cook fresh or frozen Brussels sprouts as usual, or use canned small Brussels sprouts. Skewer, and dip in melted butter combined with a little lemon juice. Sprinkle lightly with paprika and grill over medium coals 3 to 4 minutes, turning to brown evenly.

MUSHROOMS

Wash mushrooms. Peel if necessary. Sauté in butter for 4 or 5 minutes. Skewer carefully (mushrooms split easily) and grill over medium coals 3 to 4 minutes, brushing with butter and turning to brown evenly.

SMALL WHITE ONIONS

Parboil unpeeled small onions 6 to 8 minutes. Drain, cool and slip off peels. Season with salt and pepper and brush with olive oil or melted butter. Skewer, and grill over medium coals 5 to 6 minutes, turning and basting.

GREEN PEPPERS

Stem, seed and cut peppers into 1½-inch squares. Parboil gently for 3 minutes, drain and dry. Brush with melted butter or meat marinade. Skewer, and grill for 3 or 4 minutes over medium coals.

SWEET POTATOES

Parboil in jackets until almost tender. Peel. Slice thick or cut into cubes. Brush with melted butter or meat glaze. Skewer or grill in hand-grill over medium coals for 2 or 3 minutes on each side to brown.

EGGPLANT

Can be grilled peeled or unpeeled. Cube or slice, salt heavily and let stand at least a half hour. Rinse well, dry, skewer, brush with melted butter, olive oil or meat marinade and grill over medium coals for 5 or 6 minutes.

CUCUMBER

Use small firm cucumbers without large pulpy, seedy centers. Peel and cut in ¾- to 1-inch slices, season and brush with melted butter, olive oil or seasoned meat marinade. Skewer, and grill over medium coals for 3 or 4 minutes, turning to brown evenly.

Fruit for Kebabs

Many kinds of fresh and canned fruit are ideal accompaniments for meat, seafood and fowl.

However, most meat needs to be grilled longer than most fruit. Because of the natural sugar in fruit or the syrup in which it is preserved, it tends to burn more quickly than meat.

Also, as fruit grills, it softens and exudes juice, and when pressed against meat on the skewer will tend to make that part of the meat soggy and prevent its browning and crisping as it should when charcoal-broiled.

In hibachi cooking, there is the additional factor of space. It is much better to have enough room to cook the meat properly.

For these reasons, even though putting meat and fruit on the same skewer is esthetically pleasing, the food is often better when skewered separately.

Fresh or canned pineapple is an excellent fruit for grilling. It is tasty and goes with anything, but it can be overused. There are many other fruits which you can try—kumquats, apricots, plums, mango, papaya, loquats, spiced crab apples, oranges, Mandarin oranges, brandied peaches, bananas, pears, seedless grapes, Concord grapes and nectarines are a few.

MEAT

Meat

Beef

The more tender the beef, the better the finished product, but this does not mean you always have to buy the most expensive cut. Tell your butcher what you want the meat for and he may help with a suggestion. Certain cuts such as flank or skirt steaks are tender when carved at a 45° angle across the grain of the meat. Also, a natural tenderizing process takes place when meat is marinated in wine, vinegar, lemon, lime or other fruit juices. There are also commercial tenderizers which break down the connective tissues of less expensive cuts of meat.

When a recipe calls for very thin strips or slices of meat, trim the piece of meat, partially freeze it, then slice with a very sharp knife. Thaw slices completely before cooking.

Ground beef should be lean. It can be chuck, round steak or more expensive cuts, according to taste.

Lamb

The best meat for broiling on skewers is leg of lamb. Have the butcher bone and trim it well. Rib or loin chops are best for grilling.

Veal

For hibachi purposes, the best veal is from a milk-fed calf 1 to 3 months old. The meat should be fine-grained, smooth and very pale pink. Veal is always lean and must be basted frequently when grilled.

Pork

Pork must be cooked thoroughly. When it is properly done, the meat is white. It should never be served pink. Spareribs should be partially precooked and finished over charcoal. Ham steaks or cubes should be cut from a lean ready-to-eat ham.

STEAK KEBABS WITH KUMQUATS AND GREEN PEPPERS

2 *lbs. tender beef steak,*
trimmed and cut into
1½-inch cubes
2 *green peppers, seeded, cut*
into 1½-inch squares
1 *jar (8 oz. or more)*
preserved kumquats
in syrup

Marinade:
⅓ *cup soy sauce*
⅓ *cup kumquat syrup (from*
preserves)
¼ *cup sesame oil*
1 *Tbsp. light molasses*
1 *tsp. crushed red peppers*
½ *tsp. powdered ginger*
juice of 1 lemon
4 *scallions, including green*
stems, minced

Combine marinade ingredients. Pour over steak cubes and marinate for at least an hour, turning several times.

Parboil green peppers for 5 minutes.

Drain meat and skewer, alternating with kumquats and green pepper.

On oiled grill over high bed of hot coals, grill 10 to 12 minutes, turning and basting with marinade.

Note: Sesame oil is available in many specialty shops and in most Oriental food shops. It adds such an unusual nutty flavor to food that it is worth trying to get a bottle. However, if you are not able to, try this substitute:

Toast ¼ cup of sesame seeds in an ungreased skillet, stirring, until they are brown. Crush with a rolling pin, or blend in the blender with cover on. Mix crushed, toasted seeds with ½ cup of peanut oil.

SKEWERED STEAK WITH PINEAPPLE AND MUSHROOMS
(Teriyaki)

2 lbs. tender beefsteak, in
    ½-inch-thick slices
    (sirloin, cross rib, rib
    steak)
12 slices (⅛-inch) green
    ginger root (optional)
2 Tbsps. sherry
½ lb. mushrooms
1 medium-size can pineapple
    spears

Marinade:
2 tsps. minced ginger root
    or ½ tsp. powdered ginger
⅓ cup sherry
½ tsp. pepper
1 cup soy sauce
⅓ cup syrup from pineapple
2 Tbsps. brown sugar
1 onion, grated
1 clove garlic, minced fine

Bone and trim meat. Cut into 1-inch squares.

Peel green ginger root, slice and marinate in sherry to cover. Wash, trim and, if necessary, peel mushrooms.

Combine marinade ingredients and pour over steak. Marinate for several hours or overnight in refrigerator in covered non-metal container. Remove from refrigerator at least 1 hour before grilling.

Drain steak and skewer with mushrooms, ginger root and pineapple. Do not crowd pineapple against meat, because it makes meat soggy. Skewer pineapple between ginger and mushrooms or do it on a separate skewer.

Grill over hot bed of coals, turning and basting, for 4 or 5 minutes.

If you prefer this with a sauce, reserve a little of the marinade. Thicken the reserved marinade with 1 teaspoon corn-starch, simmer over low heat for 10 minutes, and keep hot while grilling meat.

SKEWERED STEAK STRIPS

2-lb. piece of tenderloin
½ cup light rum
¼ cup soy sauce
¼ cup unsweetened
    pineapple juice
2 Tbsps. lemon juice

1 tsp. dry mustard
1 Tbsp. dark molasses
1 Tbsp. minced ginger root
1 garlic clove
½ tsp. crushed red pepper

Carve diagonal strips of tenderloin, ⅛-inch thick. Marinate for 4 hours in a combination of remaining ingredients.

Thread on oiled skewers and broil 1 minute on each side over hot coals.

Serves 4.

BEEF CUBES OREGANO WITH ONIONS

2½-3 lbs. sirloin
    trimmed and cut into
    1½-inch cubes
12 small white onions,
    parboiled 10 minutes
    and peeled

Marinade:
1 clove garlic, pressed
1 tsp. salt
½ cup olive oil
¼ cup dry red wine
6 peppercorns, crushed
1 Tbsp. oregano

Mash garlic together with salt. Mix thoroughly with rest of marinade ingredients, rub well into steak cubes. Cover and refrigerate overnight. Leave at room temperature at least 1 hour before grilling. Drain and skewer, alternating several pieces of meat with 1 onion.

Over high bed of glowing coals, grill meat for 7 or 8 minutes. Turn frequently, basting with marinade.

GINGERED BEEF STRIPS WITH OYSTER SAUCE
(SKILLET)

1½ lbs. sirloin (trimmed
    weight)
1 tsp. MSG or Accent
½ tsp. black pepper, coarsely
    ground
6 dried mushrooms
    or ¼ lb. fresh mushrooms,
    sliced thin
1 medium-size cucumber
1 small can bamboo shoots,
    sliced

4 scallions
2 stalks crisp celery
4 Tbsps. peanut oil
3 slices fresh ginger root
    or ½ tsp. powdered ginger
1 Tbsp. soy sauce
4 Tbsps. oyster sauce
    (available in Oriental
    food shops)

With a sharp knife, slice meat across the grain into very
thin strips. Meat is much easier to slice thin when it is partially frozen. Thaw completely before cooking. Sprinkle meat
strips with MSG or Accent and black pepper.

VEGETABLES: Pour boiling water over dried mushrooms,
steep for 30 minutes. Squeeze out water, remove pulpy stem
and cut into thin strips. Peel cucumber and quarter, lengthwise. Remove seeds and cut into ½-inch diagonal pieces.
Drain and rinse bamboo slices. Cut scallions and celery into
thin diagonal slices.

Place skillet on grill over high bed of glowing coals. Add
2 tablespoons peanut oil. When very hot, place steak strips
in pan in a single layer. Repeat until all strips are done.
Brown *quickly* on both sides and transfer to heated platter.
Do not overcook!

Add and heat remaining peanut oil. Press ginger root
through a garlic press directly into pan, or stir in powdered
ginger. Stir once and immediately add thinly sliced scallions,
celery and cucumber. Stir 2 minutes, then add bamboo shoots
and mushrooms. Cook, stirring, 1 minute. Stir in soy sauce
and oyster sauce. Return meat slices to pan. Mix with vegetables. When everything is bubbling hot, serve at once.

BAY LEAF STEAK

4 small tender boned steaks,
   ¾ to 1 inch thick
2 oz. melted butter

Marinade:
¼ cup dry red wine
¼ cup red wine vinegar
4 bay leaves, crushed
½ tsp. salt
½ tsp. black pepper

Trim steak and steep overnight in combined wine, vinegar, crushed bay leaves and salt and pepper. Remove from refrigerator at least 1 hour before grilling. Bring to grill in marinade. Lift from marinade directly to grill.

On well-oiled grill over high hot bed of coals, grill 3 or 4 minutes on each side, brushing again with marinade when you turn.

Serve at once, pouring a little melted butter on each steak.

ROQUEFORT STEAKS

4 small tender boneless
   steaks, ¾ to 1 inch thick
¼ lb. Roquefort cheese
2 Tbsps. butter
2 Tbsps. heavy cream

1 small onion, grated
2 Tbsps. lemon juice
⅛ tsp. cayenne
1 Tbsp. Worcestershire sauce

Allow Roquefort and butter to soften at room temperature. Add heavy cream and blend until smooth, then stir in grated onion, lemon juice, cayenne and Worcestershire sauce.

Spread both sides of each steak with cheese blend. Stack steaks, one on top of the other, and let stand overnight, if possible, to absorb flavor. Remove from refrigerator at least an hour before grilling.

On well-oiled grill over high hot bed of coals, grill no more than 4 minutes on each side. (If you prefer better done steak, test and grill longer, according to taste.)

CHARCOAL-GRILLED TENDERLOIN OF BEEF

1 *whole tenderloin (5 to 6
    lbs.)*
4 *Tbsps. coarsely ground
    black pepper*

1 *Bermuda onion, sliced*
½ *cup dry red wine*
¼ *cup olive oil*
2 *oz. melted sweet butter*

Have butcher remove outside fat. He should fold over thin end of tenderloin and tie so that fillet is of uniform thickness. Meat will be tastier if he lards it in 3 or 4 places.

Press 4 tablespoons coarsely ground pepper into steak with heel of hand. Place tenderloin in shallow glass or pottery dish. Combine Bermuda onion with red wine and olive oil. Pour over steak and allow to stand at room temperature for at least 1 hour before grilling.

Grill over high bed of hot coals, turning frequently and brushing with melted butter. If you like steak rare, total cooking time will be about 25 minutes.

Remove to large platter; carve diagonally into thick slices.

GRILLED TENDERLOIN SLICES
WITH MARJORAM

4 *center slices tenderloin of
    beef, 1 inch thick*
1 *tsp. coarsely ground pepper*
2 *Tbsps. minced fresh
    marjoram*
  *or 1 Tbsp. dried marjoram
    leaves or powder*

½ *tsp. paprika*
4 *oz. sweet butter*
6 *slices French bread, ½ inch
    thick*
½ *tsp. salt*

Press coarse pepper into tenderloin slices with fingers and heel of hand.

Blend marjoram and paprika into butter softened at room temperature. Trim pieces of French bread to size of tenderloin slice, then generously spread each side of bread with herb butter.

Oil 2 long metal skewers and alternately thread bread and tenderloin until there are 3 pieces of bread and 2 of meat on each skewer.

Have a good solid bed of hot coals. Meat should be 2 or 3 inches from coals. Remove grill from hibachi top. Balance skewers on edges of hibachi. Baste with herb butter and turn to brown evenly. Grill no more than 10 minutes in all so that steaks are rare inside and crusty outside. Salt and serve.

RUMANIAN FLANK STEAK

1 fat flank steak,
    approximately 1½ lbs.
1 tsp. coarsely ground pepper

¼ cup olive oil
1 clove garlic, pressed

With a sharp knife, score steak lightly on each side. Sprinkle with pepper. Dip steak into olive oil mixed with garlic.

On well-oiled grill over very hot coals, grill steak no more than 3 minutes on each side, basting with oil when you turn.

IMPORTANT: Carving is the key to tender flank steak. Cut into very thin slices, with the knife blade at a 45° angle.

MARINATED FLANK STEAK, GRILLED

1 fat flank steak
    approximately 1½ lbs.

Marinade:
4 Tbsps. lemon or lime juice
3 Tbsps. honey
¼ cup soy sauce
2 scallions, finely chopped
2 Tbsps. sesame oil

With a sharp knife, score steak lightly on each side. Marinate overnight in combined marinade ingredients, turning once or twice.

On well-oiled grill over very hot coals, grill steak no more than 3 minutes on each side, basting with marinade.

Cut the meat into very thin slices, with the knife blade at a 45° angle.

SHELL STEAK AU POIVRE

1 *steak per person*
   (*cut ½ to ¾ inches*
   thick)
4 *Tbsps. whole*
   peppercorns }*for 4 steaks*
4 *Tbsps. brandy*
	Sauce: (*for 4*)
	6 *Tbsps. butter*
	2 or 3 *drops Tabasco sauce*
	2 *Tbsps. lemon juice*
	1 *Tbsp. Worcestershire sauce*
	2 *Tbsps. chopped chives*
	2 *Tbsps. chopped parsley*

Crush peppercorns until they are completely cracked. (Use a mortar and pestle, a rolling pin on a wooden board, or place them between 2 sheets of heavy brown paper and pound with a mallet.) Put in a small jar and pour in brandy. This will keep for a long time in refrigerator, and should be done well ahead of time.

Trim excess fat from steaks and cut small incisions around edge to prevent curling. Blot meat with paper towels. Press cracked peppercorns into both sides of steaks, using fingers and heel of hands to work the pepper into the meat. Cover meat with waxed paper or plastic wrap and store in refrigerator overnight. Remove to room temperature at least an hour before grilling.

Shortly before grill-time, melt butter, add Tabasco, lemon juice and Worcestershire. Keep warm. At last minute, blot steaks again with paper towels.

Place steaks on well-oiled grill over high bed of hot coals. Grill no more than 3 or 4 minutes on each side. Stir chopped chives and parsley into seasoned lemon-butter sauce. Remove steaks to platter, pour sauce over all and serve at once.

CUBE STEAKS CARIBBEAN

8 *small cube or minute steaks*
3 *Tbsps. grated orange rind*
½ *cup orange juice*
½ *clove garlic, pressed*
½ *tsp. grated nutmeg*

1 *tsp. coarsely ground pepper*
1 *whole orange, with skin,*
    sliced thin
4 *Tbsps. olive oil*
8 *thin pats of butter*

Combine grated rind and juice of oranges with garlic and nutmeg. Season steaks with pepper.

Pour in just enough seasoned orange juice to cover bottom of a glass dish (large enough to lay 1 steak out flat and deep enough to accommodate the 8 steaks stacked, one on top of the other). Arrange steak stack as follows: 1 steak, thin slice of whole orange, some of the juice, another steak, etc. Then cover top of dish with wax paper or plastic wrap and refrigerate overnight.

Drain steaks and discard orange slices. Brush well with olive oil. On a well-oiled grill over a deep hot bed of glowing coals grill steaks quickly, no more than ½ minute on each side. Remove to serving platter, sprinkle lightly with salt, and serve with a thin pat of butter on each steak.

STEAK DIANE
(SKILLET)

2 *lbs. tender steak (sirloin,*
    Delmonico, porterhouse)
small piece of beef suet
6 *Tbsps. melted sweet butter*

4 *Tbsps. finely chopped*
    chives
4 *Tbsps. dry sherry*
3 *Tbsps. cognac, warmed*

Have steak trimmed, boned and sliced in ¼-inch slices, then pounded very thin.

Heat heavy skillet over high bed of glowing coals. Rub skillet quickly with beef suet (hold suet with tongs) to grease slightly. When skillet is very hot, prepare steaks as follows:

Holding steak with tongs, *quickly* sear one side, then the other (just long enough to brown). Remove slice to hot platter and repeat until all meat has been cooked.

Add melted butter, chives and sherry to skillet. Stir, scraping pan to loosen all brown bits, until heated through. Return steaks to skillet to coat with sauce.

Add 3 tablespoons warmed cognac, set aflame. Serve at once.

HIBACHI STROGANOFF
(SKILLET)

1½ lbs. beef tenderloin
  or *other tender cut of solid*
    beef
½ tsp. salt
½ tsp. *white pepper*
2 *Tbsps. paprika*
½ lb. *fresh mushrooms*

8 *shallots*
  or 2 *small onions*
small piece of beef suet
2 *Tbsps. butter*
1 *clove garlic*
1 *cup heavy cream*

Slice beef tenderloin in very thin strips across the grain. This is easier if meat is partially frozen. Season strips with salt, pepper and paprika. Allow to thaw completely at room temperature.

Clean and trim mushrooms, peeling if necessary. Slice thin. Mince shallots or onions.

In heavy skillet over hot bed of coals, render beef suet. Add 2 tablespoons of butter and when hot, squeeze garlic clove through press directly into skillet. Add beef slices, 6 or 8 at a time, brown very quickly on both sides and remove immediately to hot plate. Repeat until all the beef is browned. Add shallots and mushrooms and sauté, stirring, for 2 minutes. Return meat to skillet and mix with mushrooms and shallots. Stir in cup of warm heavy cream. Correct seasoning and simmer, stirring, until very hot, but not boiling. Meat should not be overcooked.

Sukiyaki

In a Japanese book published nearly two centuries ago, this description of sukiyaki was given: "To grill chicken, seasoned in soy, on a plowshare over a fire," but the theories and legends about the origin of sukiyaki are as varied as the recipes for it are today. However, there seems to be little doubt that it has been served in Japan for more than a hundred years and is becoming increasingly popular in other parts of the world.

The Japanese make a charming ritual of preparing and eating sukiyaki. They sit on the floor on cushions around a beautiful array of the sukiyaki ingredients, with the thick iron pan or *nabe* atop the glowing charcoal fire of the hibachi. Each person has an individual tray set with chopsticks, rice bowl and dishes for broth and sauces.

There is a difference of opinion, even among such experts, as to which foods go into the pan first. Some prefer to select some of the meat first, dipping it in soy sauce, then into the pan for a quick searing, then into a hot mustard sauce or beaten raw egg. Others prefer to cook the vegetables first, and add the liquids and meats later. In other words there is no absolute rule about procedure.

Most Westerners prefer to sit on chairs at a table but we can still have an attractive arrangement of ingredients and the hibachi, and retain the custom of a leisurely, pleasant meal.

A NOTE ON THE INGREDIENTS: All the ingredients for sukiyaki listed below are available in Oriental grocery stores; many of them are in supermarkets or specialty shops.

Shirataki, sometimes called "cellophane noodles," are thin noodles resembling vermicelli. One variety is available in tins. Another variety, dried, should be dropped into boiling water, the flame turned off and the noodles left in the water for 30 minutes. If shirataki are unavailable, you can substitute cold cooked vermicelli.

Tofu is soy bean curd which is available at Oriental groceries in bulk or in cans.

Bean Sprouts are much better fresh but are sold in cans. If you use canned bean sprouts, rinse them thoroughly and let them stand covered with ice water for a half hour before using.

Sake is Japanese rice wine, and it is available in some liquor stores. Sherry is the most common substitute, but you can use white wine, vermouth or even beer.

Shoyu or *Soy Sauce* is a very important ingredient, and should be of good quality. The Japanese or Chinese types are much less expensive if you buy a pint or quart-size bottle. It will keep indefinitely.

Bamboo Shoots come in cans of various sizes, and they are available sliced or whole.

Dried Mushrooms come in a variety of types, and add an entirely different flavor to food. If unavailable, substitute fresh or canned button or sliced mushrooms.

Sugar: Japanese use sugar whenever they use soy sauce, but they use much more than most Americans do. They would use ⅓ cup sugar to ½ cup of soy sauce and ¼ cup sake. *Add* more sugar later, if you like, but start with the amount indicated in the recipe.

BEEF SUKIYAKI

(SKILLET)

2 lbs. tender beef, sliced thin
1 tsp. MSG, Accent or
    Ajinomoto
½ oz. dried mushrooms
    or ½ lb. fresh mushrooms
½ Chinese cabbage
½ lb. fresh young spinach
    leaves
12 half-inch cubes of tofu or
    bean curd
½ cup fresh or canned bean
    sprouts
3 tender inner stalks of celery
2 leeks
1 bunch scallions
2 oz. beef suet, cut in 4 or 5
    pieces

1 cup shirataki ("cellophane
    noodles")
    or cold cooked vermicelli
1 5-oz. can sliced bamboo
    shoots
1½ cups beef bouillon

Sauce:
½ cup soy sauce
¼ cup sake, sherry or
    vermouth
¼ cup water
2 Tbsps. sugar
½ tsp. pepper

MEAT: Use a tender cut of beef—boned rib roast, shoulder steak, sirloin, face rump, skirt steak or fillet. Ask your butcher to machine-slice the meat paper thin. If this cannot be arranged, partially freeze the meat and slice it as thin as you can. Sprinkle it with MSG and thaw completely.

VEGETABLES: Pour boiling water over dried mushrooms, soak at least 30 minutes, squeeze out moisture, trim stems and slice thin.

Cut Chinese cabbage in 1-inch lengths.

Wash spinach thoroughly, discard stems, and steam for a few minutes with the water that clings to the leaves, in order to reduce bulk.

Cut bean curd in ½-inch cubes, handling carefully to avoid breaking.

If you use fresh bean sprouts, wash and drain them. If you use canned bean sprouts, drain them, rinse with cold water and soak in ice water at least ½ hour.

Cut celery diagonally in thin slices.

Slice leeks thin.

Cut scallions, including some of the green part, in ½-inch pieces.

Place a heavy iron skillet on the grill of the hibachi over a high hot bed of glowing coals. When the skillet is very hot, melt a piece of the beef suet.

IMPORTANT: Meat should not be overcooked and vegetables should be crisp; the sukiyaki should be eaten hot, and in a leisurely manner. Do not try to cook everything at once. Each ingredient should be in a separate pile or dish. Select portions of each to start with, and add to the pan as needed.

Into the hot suet in the pan put some of the leeks, scallions, mushrooms and celery. Cook, stirring, for 2 minutes. Push to one side of the skillet.

Combine the soy sauce, wine, water, sugar and pepper. Pour in enough of this sauce to cover the bottom of the skillet. When it is hot add a layer of beef slices and cook only until the beef turns color. Turn with tongs or spatula, cook briefly, and lay on top of the vegetables at the side of the skillet. Repeat with another layer of meat. Mix the vegetables and meat together in the middle of the pan and add proportionate amounts of cabbage, bean curd, spinach, shirataki, bean sprouts and bamboo shoots. Add half the bouillon and some of the soy mixture. Stir gently several times, bringing the meat to the top whenever possible. Let simmer for 6 or 7 minutes, until everything is heated thoroughly. Serve in deep plates or soup bowls with boiled white rice on the side.

Keep the skillet hot on the hibachi. Add more bouillon and soy sauce thinned with a little water, and add meat and vegetables as you wish.

GRILLED HAMBURGER — VARIATIONS

Each of the following recipes is for 1 pound of lean beef, ground. After combining ingredients with beef, form into 4 patties and chill. When ready to grill, place patties in oiled hand-grill and grill 4 or 5 minutes on each side over hot coals.

To BEEF ADD:
1 *onion, grated fine*
1 *medium raw potato, grated and drained*
1 *Tbsp. chopped parsley*
½ *tsp. salt*
¼ *tsp. black pepper*
1 *Tbsp. Worcestershire sauce*

To BEEF ADD:
2 *Tbsps. capers, rinsed and mashed*
2 *Tbsps. chopped chives*
3 *Tbsps. finely chopped almonds*
¼ *tsp. powdered saffron*
½ *tsp. salt*
1 *slightly beaten egg*

To BEEF ADD:
2 *Tbsps. finely chopped fresh dill*
2 *Tbsps. chopped chives*
½ *tsp. salt*
6 *stuffed green olives, sliced thin*
2 *hard-cooked egg yolks, sieved*
1 *Tbsp. tomato paste*
1 or 2 *Tbsps. ice water*

To BEEF ADD:
½ *cup minced raw mushrooms*
½ *tsp. ground juniper berries*
2 *Tbsps. dry vermouth*
½ *tsp. salt*
2 *Tbsps. minced chives*

BEEFBURGERS WITH SOUR CREAM AND RED CAVIAR

1 *lb. ground lean beef*
1 *onion, chopped fine*
6 *to 8 fresh mushrooms, diced fine*
3 *Tbsps. butter*
1 *tsp. paprika*

½ *tsp. salt*
¼ *tsp. black pepper*
pinch of cayenne pepper
½ *cup sour cream*
2 *oz. red caviar*

Sauté onion and mushrooms in 1 tablespoon butter for 5 minutes. Season with paprika, salt, pepper and cayenne. Remove from heat and cool. Stir in 3 tablespoons sour cream. Blend with ground meat. Form into 4 patties. Chill.

Brush patties with melted butter. Place in oiled hand-grill. Remove grid from hibachi and grill over hot coals, 4 or 5 minutes on each side.

Remove to heated platter. Spoon generous portion of sour cream, topped by a spoonful of red caviar, onto each patty.

GRILLED CHOPPED BEEF WITH FRESH GREENS

2 *lbs. lean beef, ground*
2 *eggs, slightly beaten*
¼ *cup chopped parsley*
½ *cup chopped watercress (leaves only)*
5 *Tbsps. chopped chives*

1 *Tbsp. capers*
1 *tsp. salt*
1 *tsp. black pepper*
4 *Tbsps. dry red wine*
2 *Tbsps. olive oil*
4 *Tbsps. melted butter*

Combine ground beef, eggs, parsley, watercress, 4 tablespoons chives, capers, salt and pepper. Mix lightly but thoroughly; add wine, oil; blend. Form into 8 patties, chill.

Combine butter and 1 tablespoon chives and brush on patties. Place in oiled hand-grill. Remove grid from hibachi and grill over hot coals, 4 or 5 minutes on each side, basting with butter sauce. Turn only once.

CHEDDARBURGERS

2 lbs. lean beef, ground
6 slices bacon
6 small scallions, minced
1 tsp. freshly ground black
    pepper
½ cup grated sharp Cheddar
    cheese

2 Tbsps. Worcestershire
    sauce
2 Tbsps. chili sauce
2 or 3 Tbsps. cold tomato
    juice

Pan-fry bacon until crisp. Remove to paper towel, blot, and crumble fine.

Drain off all but 1 tablespoon bacon fat from pan and sauté scallions for 5 minutes.

Combine ground beef, pepper, bacon crumbles and scallions. Add grated cheese, Worcestershire and chili sauce. Add tomato juice. Form into 8 uniform patties. Chill.

Brush patties with bacon fat and place in oiled hand-grill. Remove grid from hibachi and grill over hot coals, 4 or 5 minutes on each side, turning only once.

GRILLED BEEF AND MARROW

1½ lbs. lean beef, ground
4 oz. beef marrow, chopped
    fine
1 tsp. salt
1 tsp. black pepper

⅛ tsp. nutmeg
4 Tbsps. chopped chives
3 Tbsps. ice water
6 Tbsps. melted butter
2 Tbsps. lime juice

Season ground beef and chopped marrow with salt, pepper and nutmeg. Mix in chopped chives, then ice water. Form into 8 uniform patties and chill thoroughly.

Remove from refrigerator just before grilling. Combine butter and lime juice and brush on patties. Place in oiled hand-grill. Remove grid from hibachi and grill patties over hot coals for 5 or 6 minutes on each side, basting with lime butter.

PÂTÉ BURGERS

2 lbs. lean beef, ground
½ tsp. salt
1 tsp. black pepper
2 cans (about 3 oz. each)
    pâté with truffles

1 cup dry red wine
3 oz. melted butter

Season ground beef with salt and pepper and combine with pâté. Handling very lightly, form into 8 patties. Lay on a deep glass or china platter. Make a small indentation in the center of each patty and fill with red wine. Pour remainder of wine over all and chill in refrigerator 2 or 3 hours.

Just before grilling, remove from refrigerator, pour off wine, brush with melted butter and place on oiled hand-grill. Grill over medium hot coals (with hibachi grid removed) for 4 to 5 minutes on each side.

MEXICAN BURGERS

2 lbs. lean beef, ground
1 tsp. salt
½ clove garlic, pressed
1 Tbsp. chili powder
1 tsp. black pepper
1 medium onion, grated

2 Tbsps. olive oil
2 Tbsps. dry red wine
¼ cup melted butter
¼ cup lime juice
½ tsp. crushed red peppers

Mix salt and garlic together with chili powder and black pepper. Add grated onion and blend with oil and wine. Mix thoroughly with ground beef. Form into 8 patties. Chill.

Combine melted butter, lime juice and crushed red peppers for basting sauce.

In oiled hand-grill over hot coals, grill patties for 4 or 5 minutes, basting with lime-butter sauce. Turn, baste, and grill for an additional 4 or 5 minutes.

COFFEEBURGERS WITH BLEU CHEESE

2 lbs. lean beef, ground
1/3 lb. bleu cheese
1 medium onion, grated
2 Tbsps. chopped parsley
2 tsps. paprika

3-4 Tbsps. strong cold black
     coffee
1 tsp. salt
1/2 tsp. black pepper
2-3 dashes Angostura bitters
2 oz. melted butter

Bring bleu cheese to room temperature. Work into a smooth paste with grated onion and parsley. Blend in paprika. Add enough black coffee to make a spreading consistency.

Season ground beef with salt, pepper and bitters. Form into 12 thin patties. Spread a generous layer of cheese mixture on 6 of the patties, top with the other 6, pressing edges together. Chill.

Brush patties on each side with melted butter, and place on an oiled hand-grill. Remove grid from hibachi and grill over medium hot coals for 5 or 6 minutes on each side, turning only once.

Serve plain—or on toasted crisp rolls with thin slices of red onion.

PEANUT BURGERS

2 lbs. lean beef, ground
1/2 cup minced onion
2 Tbsps. butter
1 tsp. fresh ginger, pressed
   or 1/4 tsp. powdered ginger
1 tsp. black pepper

1/2 cup roasted peanuts,
     coarsely ground
1/4 cup soy sauce
2 Tbsps. sherry
1 tsp. brown sugar
1 Tbsp. sesame oil

Sauté onions in butter for 5 minutes. Stir in ginger and black pepper. Remove from heat and mix with peanuts.

Combine soy sauce, sherry, brown sugar and sesame oil.

Add 2 tablespoons of this to onion-peanut mixture and combine with ground meat. Handling lightly, form into 8 uniform patties. Pour remaining soy-sherry sauce over patties and chill until ready to grill.

Remove patties from sauce. In oiled hand-grill over hot coals, grill for 4 or 5 minutes on each side, basting with sauce.

GRILLED CHINESE HAMBURGERS

2 lbs. ground lean chuck or
    top round steak
2 Tbsps. soy sauce
1 medium green pepper,
    chopped fine
1 medium onion, chopped
    fine

6 water chestnuts, diced
1 small can shrimp
    or 8 large cooked shrimp,
      cut fine
½ tsp. Accent
salt and pepper to taste
2 eggs

Combine all above ingredients except eggs and blend thoroughly with wooden spoon or hands. Add eggs; Mix well.

Handling lightly, form into 8 patties approximately ½ inch thick. Broil in oiled hand-grill over hot charcoals, 5 or 6 minutes on each side.

"HERO" BURGERS

1½ lbs. lean beef, ground
4 Tbsps. olive oil
2 large onions, chopped
1 large green pepper, sliced
    thin
1 clove garlic, pressed
¼ lb. mushrooms, sliced
½ lb. hot Italian sausage,
    cut up
3 Tbsps. chopped parsley
2 Tbsps. tomato paste

1 medium-size can Italian
    plum tomatoes
1½ tsps. oregano
1 tsp. sweet basil
¼ tsp. grated nutmeg
¼ tsp. crushed anise seeds
1 tsp. salt
1 egg, slightly beaten
½ lb. mozzarella cheese
4 small French or Italian
    breads or grinder rolls

Sauce can be made a day ahead. Heat 2 tablespoons olive oil in large, heavy skillet. Sauté onions, green pepper, garlic and mushrooms until soft. Add sausages and brown. Stir in chopped parsley, tomato paste, tomatoes, oregano, basil, nutmeg, crushed anise seeds and salt. Simmer slowly, covered, for at least an hour. Correct seasoning and allow to cool.

Combine ground beef with ¼ cup sauce and beaten egg. Divide into 4 portions and shape into thick rectangular form to fit grinder roll.

Cut mozzarella cheese into small pieces and press a number of cheese bits into meat. Cover burgers with wax paper and chill until ready to grill.

Reheat sauce and keep hot over very low flame.

At grilling time, remove burgers from refrigerator, brush with olive oil, and place in oiled basket-type hand-grill. Remove grid from hibachi and grill over hot coals for 6 to 8 minutes on each side, turning only once.

Lay a patty on each heated, split grinder roll. Ladle lavish portions of hot sauce over each burger. Serve on large plates. Don't forget to have plenty of paper napkins or damp hand towels.

GREEK MEATBALLS, GRILLED

1 lb. lean pork, ground	½ tsp. black pepper
1 lb. beef, ground	1 tsp. cinnamon
2 Tbsps. olive oil	1 tsp. allspice
1 clove garlic, pressed	2 Tbsps. grated orange rind
12 black Greek olives, chopped fine	¼ cup orange juice
	¼ cup dry red wine
1 tsp. salt	3 Tbsps. lemon juice

SPECIAL NOTE: Because pork needs longer cooking, precook it before combining with the other ingredients. Sauté ground pork slowly in olive oil for 30 minutes. Cool.

Combine sautéed pork with ground beef, garlic and chopped olives. Season with salt, pepper, cinnamon, allspice

and grated orange rind. Add orange juice and wine. Mix well
and chill for 3 or 4 hours.

At grilling time, remove meat from refrigerator. Apply a
small amount of olive oil to hands and shape meat into
walnut-size meatballs. String onto thin skewers, leaving small
space between meatballs.

On oiled grill over high bed of hot coals, grill meatballs,
turning to brown all sides. Grill for a total of 4 or 5 minutes.
Remove to platter.

Sprinkle with lemon juice and serve at once.

TWO-WAY LITTLE MEATBALLS, ITALIAN STYLE
(IN THE SKILLET—OR ON THE GRILL)

1½ lbs. lean beef, ground
    twice
½ lb. veal, ground
6 slices lean bacon, cooked
    crisp and crumbled fine
½ cup bread crumbs, soaked
    in milk and squeezed
    dry
1 clove garlic, pressed
1 Tbsp. grated lemon rind

¼ cup seedless raisins,
    soaked in wine and
    chopped
2 Tbsps. finely chopped
    parsley
salt
1 tsp. black pepper
2 large eggs, slightly beaten
olive oil

Combine ground beef and veal with crumbled bacon, bread
crumbs, garlic, lemon rind, raisins and parsley. Season with
salt and pepper. Stir in beaten eggs and work mixture until
smooth.

Apply small amount of olive oil to hands and form mixture
into bite-size meatballs.

To GRILL: Skewer on thin metal or well-soaked bamboo
skewers, brush with olive oil and grill for 2 or 3 minutes over
hot coals, turning to brown evenly.

IN SKILLET: Heat 2 or 3 tablespoons olive oil in heavy skillet
over hot charcoal bed. Cook meatballs, not too many at a time,
turning to brown all sides. Remove with slotted spoon to

heated platter. Add more oil to pan as needed. Serve hot.

This recipe will serve 4 to 6 as a main course; 12 or more as appetizers.

GRILLED VEAL CHOPS

4 loin veal chops, cut 1 inch
   thick
2 Tbsps. lemon juice

2 Tbsps. chopped chives
6 Tbsps. melted butter
salt and pepper

Combine lemon juice and chives with melted butter. Season veal chops with salt and pepper and brush well with butter sauce.

Adjust grill of hibachi to second level over a hot bed of coals. Veal needs to be basted often during grilling to keep it from becoming too dry. Grill chops for 10 to 12 minutes on each side, brushing on plenty of the butter sauce to keep them moist.

VEAL SCALLOPS WITH MANDARIN ORANGES AND GREEN OLIVES
(SKILLET)

1½ lbs. veal scallops, cut
   thin and pounded
   thinner
½ tsp. salt
½ tsp. freshly ground black
   pepper
1 can Mandarin orange
   segments

2 Tbsps. olive oil
2 Tbsps. butter
½ cup beef consommé
8 pitted green olives, sliced
   thin
2 Tbsps. chopped parsley

Cut pounded scallops into pieces about 3 inches square. Sprinkle with salt and pepper. Drain Mandarin orange segments, reserving juice.

In a heavy skillet, over high hot bed of glowing coals, heat olive oil and butter. Quickly brown veal scallops (no more than 1 or 2 minutes on each side) and remove to heated platter.

Pour consommé and juice from oranges into skillet, stirring to scrape up all brown bits from bottom and sides of pan. Add sliced olives and orange sections, heat thoroughly and pour over scallops. Sprinkle with chopped parsley and serve at once.

VEAL STRIPS WITH MUSHROOMS AND PEPPERS
(SKILLET)

1½ lbs. veal scallops, cut thin	6 shallots
3 Tbsps. flour	or 1 medium onion, minced
½ tsp. salt	½ lb. fresh mushrooms
½ tsp. pepper	3 Tbsps. butter
1 tsp. paprika	3 Tbsps. olive oil
1 medium green pepper	6 Tbsps. dry vermouth
	2 Tbsps. chopped parsley

Place veal scallops between 2 pieces of heavy waxed paper and pound thin with a rolling pin or mallet. Cut into ½-inch strips. Dredge lightly in flour combined with salt, pepper and paprika.

Seed and slice green pepper into narrow, lengthwise strips. Pour boiling water over the strips and let stand 5 minutes. Drain and dry.

Peel and slice shallots thin. Clean and trim mushrooms, peel if necessary, and slice into thin strips.

In heavy skillet over high bed of hot coals, heat 2 tablespoons each of butter and olive oil. Sauté shallots, mushrooms and green pepper for 3 minutes, stirring constantly. Remove with slotted spoon to hot platter. Add remaining oil and butter. When it is very hot, add a layer of veal strips. Cook very quickly, turning only once. Cook no more than 1 minute on each side. As veal strips are finished, remove them to hot platter with vegetables. Repeat until all meat is done. Use more butter and oil if necessary.

Pour vermouth into skillet and scrape bottom and sides of pan to loosen any brown particles. Return veal strips and vegetables to pan, mix thoroughly, and when they are very hot sprinkle with chopped parsley. Serve at once.

GRILLED VEAL CUBES WITH APRICOT SAUCE
(Sasaties—from South Africa)

2 lbs. boned veal, cut in 1-inch squares

Marinade:

1 cup dried apricots	¼ cup brown sugar
3 medium onions, chopped fine	2 Tbsps. curry powder
½ clove garlic, minced	⅛ tsp. cayenne pepper
4 Tbsps. butter	1 tsp. salt
1 cup apricot nectar	¼ cup lime or lemon juice

SAUCE: Cook dried apricots with a little water until soft. Blend with enough of the water in which they were cooked, to make a smooth purée. Sauté onions and garlic in butter until soft. Add apricot nectar and brown sugar. Heat until sugar is dissolved. Add curry powder, cayenne, salt and lime juice. Add apricot purée, simmer gently 5 minutes, cool.

Coat veal cubes thoroughly with cooled marinade. Refrigerate (in non-metal container) for 3 or 4 hours, preferably overnight. Remove from refrigerator an hour before cooking. When ready to grill, lift veal from marinade—only drain off excess, don't dry or scrape pieces. Skewer loosely on oiled skewers.

Add ½ cup cold water to remaining marinade and heat slowly.

Over a medium bed of hot coals, grill veal for 10 to 12 minutes, turning to brown all sides. Serve at once with hot apricot sauce on the side.

VEAL PATTIES WITH SMOKED OYSTERS
AND ANCHOVIES

1½ lbs. veal, ground
1 small can smoked oysters,
   in oil
2 oz. marrow, minced
1 onion, minced fine
1 Tbsp. butter

¼ tsp. white pepper
½ tsp. salt
4 Tbsps. chopped parsley
2 egg yolks, slightly beaten
6 rolled anchovy fillets,
   with capers

Drain smoked oysters, reserving oil, and mince very fine. Combine with ground veal and minced marrow.

Sauté onion in butter until soft and add to veal mixture with pepper, salt and parsley. Add beaten egg yolks. Blend well.

With a little of the oil from the oysters, oil hands and form meat into 6 uniform patties. Press a rolled anchovy fillet into center of each patty. Chill until ready to cook.

Remove patties from refrigerator, brush with a little of the oyster oil and place on well-oiled hand-grill. Grill over medium hot coals for 5 minutes on each side, turning only once.

SHASHLIK

leg of lamb, boned and cut
   into 1½-inch cubes
1 cup olive oil
1 cup dry red wine
3 Tbsps. red wine vinegar

¼ cup fresh dill, chopped
¼ cup fresh parsley, chopped
1 Tbsp. oregano
salt, pepper to taste
3 medium-size onions, sliced

Mix oil, wine and vinegar. Add dill, parsley, oregano, salt and pepper. Mix in sliced onions, add lamb cubes and coat thoroughly. Allow to marinate over night, stirring at least 4 or 5 times.

Four or 5 hours before grilling, the accompanying vegetables can be added to the marinade to absorb additional flavor.

Tiny tomatoes, mushrooms, eggplant cubes, green peppers, small white onions are all appropriate for this dish. The vegetables should be skewered and cooked a shorter time than the meat.

Place lamb cubes on skewers, allowing a ½-inch space between pieces. Broil over hot charcoals, turning frequently and brushing with marinade, about 8 to 10 minutes. Do not overcook.

Note: This marinade makes a delicious dressing for a tossed green salad.

CAUCASIAN SHASHLIK

2 lbs. boneless lamb, from leg or loin, cut into 1-inch cubes
1 large onion, sliced thin
1 clove garlic, pressed
3 Tbsps. olive oil

Marinade:
¾ cup cider vinegar
¼ cup water
6 peppercorns, crushed
1 tsp. salt
½ tsp. ground cloves
½ tsp. ground cinnamon
½ tsp. grated nutmeg
½ cup dry red wine

Trim fat and remove as much connective tissue and membrane as possible from lamb cubes. Place in bowl with onion and garlic and cover.

Combine vinegar, water, crushed peppercorns, salt, cloves, cinnamon and nutmeg in small saucepan and simmer gently for 10 minutes. Remove from fire and cool. Add wine to cooled mixture. Pour over lamb cubes, cover, and refrigerate overnight.

Remove from refrigerator an hour before using. Drain lamb, brush with olive oil and skewer.

Grill over hot coals, turning and brushing with olive oil, for 6 to 8 minutes.

SHISHKEBAB

5-6 *lb. boned leg of lamb*
½ *cup olive oil*
½ *cup lemon juice*
1 *pressed garlic clove*
1 *onion, minced*
1½ *Tbsps. salt*

1 *tsp. fresh ginger root,*
  minced
2 *tsps. coriander seeds*
2 *tsps. curry powder*
1 *tsp. turmeric*
1 *crushed cardamom seed*

Have lamb cut into 1½-inch cubes.

Marinate in combination of remaining ingredients for 12 hours or more.

Thread meat on skewers, leaving small spaces between pieces, and grill over hot coals until well browned on outside but still pink and juicy inside. This will not take more than 8 to 10 minutes' total cooking time.

MOORISH KEBABS

2 *lbs. boneless lamb, from leg or loin, cut into 1-inch cubes*

Marinade:
½ *cup olive oil*
1 *large onion, chopped fine*
1 *Tbsp. crushed cumin seed*
½ *cup finely chopped*
  parsley

2 *cloves garlic, crushed*
1 *bay leaf, crumbled*
1 *tsp. salt*
1 *tsp. black pepper*
1 *Tbsp. hot paprika*

Trim fat and remove as much connective tissue and membrane as possible from lamb cubes.

Combine all remaining ingredients (this will be very thick). Rub well into lamb cubes. Refrigerate in covered container overnight. Remove from refrigerator at least an hour before cooking.

Skewer, leaving spaces between pieces. Grill over hot coals, turning to brown evenly, 6 to 8 minutes. Don't worry if some of the marinade clings to the lamb—it will taste all the better.

ORIENTAL LAMB KEBABS

2 lbs. boneless lamb, from leg or loin, cut into 1-inch cubes
6 scallions, cut in 1-inch lengths
1 8- or 9½-oz. jar preserved kumquats, in syrup
3 Tbsps. peanut oil

Marinade:
½ cup unsweetened pineapple juice
juice from kumquat preserves
¼ cup soy sauce
1 Tbsp. sesame oil (optional)
½ clove garlic, crushed

Trim fat and remove as much connective tissue and membrane as possible from lamb cubes.

Marinate lamb cubes in combined marinade ingredients for 2 hours, turning occasionally.

Skewer drained lamb cubes, alternating with scallions and kumquats. Brush with peanut oil.

Grill over hot coals, turning and brushing with peanut oil, 6 to 8 minutes.

SHERRIED LAMB AND KIDNEY KEBABS

1½ lbs. meat from leg of
    baby lamb, cut into
    1-inch cubes
4 lamb kidneys
8 slices Canadian bacon, cut
    in 1-inch pieces
3 oz. melted butter

Marinade:
½ cup dry sherry
1 tsp. dry rosemary
½ bay leaf, crumbled
½ tsp. dry thyme
1 tsp. salt
½ tsp. pepper

Trim fat and remove as much connective tissue and membrane as possible from lamb cubes.

Remove outer skin from kidneys, slice in half lengthwise and remove hard white core with sharp knife. Then cut each half across the middle.

Combine marinade ingredients and pour over lamb and kidneys. Marinate for several hours, turning occasionally.

Drain lamb and kidneys and skewer, alternating with pieces of Canadian bacon. Brush with melted butter.

Broil over hot coals, basting with melted butter, for no more than 7 minutes in all. Lamb should be slightly pink inside. Kidneys toughen with overcooking.

SKEWERED LAMB, GREEK STYLE

2 lbs. meat from leg of baby
    lamb, cut into 1-inch
    cubes
½ cup lemon juice

1 tsp. oregano
1 tsp. salt
1 tsp. freshly ground black
    pepper

Combine lemon juice with oregano, salt and pepper.

Trim fat and remove as much connective tissue and membrane as possible from lamb cubes.

Dip lamb cubes into seasoned lemon juice and skewer.

Grill over hot charcoal, turning to brown all sides, for 6 minutes.

SKEWERED LAMB WITH LEMON AND DILL

2 lbs. meat from leg of baby
   lamb, cut in 1-inch
   cubes
1/4 cup olive oil
3 lemons, juice and grated
   rind

4 Tbsps. fresh dill, chopped
   fine
  or 2 Tbsps. dried dill weed
2 tsps. salt
1 tsp. black pepper

Trim fat and remove as much connective tissue and membrane as possible from lamb cubes.

Combine all remaining ingredients and pour over lamb cubes, turning to coat. If young lamb is used, it will have a delicate flavor after 1/2 hour of marinating.

Skewer lamb, being careful not to crowd pieces together.

Grill over hot coals for 6 to 8 minutes, basting with marinade, and turning often to brown evently. *Do not overcook.*

SKEWERED LAMB, WITH A TOUCH OF INDIA

5-lb. leg of lamb, boned, and cut into 1 1/2-inch cubes
1 cup toasted sesame seed (optional)

Marinade:
1/2 cup olive oil
1/3 cup lime or lemon juice
1 clove garlic, pressed
1 fresh red chili pepper,
   chopped fine
  or 1 tsp. crushed red pepper

1 tsp. powdered ginger
1 Tbsp. curry powder
1 tsp. freshly ground black
   pepper
1 1/2 tsp. salt

Trim fat and remove as much connective tissue and membrane as possible from lamb cubes.

Combine marinade ingredients and pour over lamb cubes in non-metal container. Marinate overnight. Turn pieces occasionally to season evenly. Remove from refrigerator at least 1 hour before grilling.

Drain lamb and, if desired, dip each piece into sesame seeds to coat. Skewer, leaving a small space between pieces.

Grill over hot coals, turning often, for a total of 8 to 10 minutes. Meat should be pink and juicy inside.

Note: To toast sesame seeds, place in a heavy skillet, ungreased, over medium heat. Stir until lightly browned.

GRILLED LAMB CUBES, RUSSIAN STYLE

2 *lbs. meat from leg of baby*
    lamb, cut into 1-inch
    cubes
1/2 *cup dry red wine*
1/4 *cup olive oil*
2 *Tbsps. red wine vinegar*

1 *tsp. salt*
1/2 *tsp. black pepper*
1/2 *clove garlic, pressed*
1/2 *tsp. dried tarragon*
1/4 *tsp. powdered cloves*

Trim fat and remove as much connective tissue and membrane as possible from lamb cubes.

Combine all remaining ingredients and pour over lamb cubes, turning to coat. Marinate for an hour, drain and skewer.

Grill over hot coals 6 to 8 minutes, turning and basting. Do not overcook.

Serves 4.

INDONESIAN SKEWERED LAMB, WITH HOT DIP
(SATÉ KAMBING)

4½ to 5-lb. leg of baby lamb, boned and cut into 1-inch cubes
1½ cups red wine vinegar
4 Tbsps. olive or peanut oil

Seasoning Paste:	Dipping Sauce:
4 Tbsps. soy sauce	1 clove garlic, minced
2 Tbsps. dark molasses	½ cup ground peanuts
1 tsp. crushed red peppers	1 tsp. crushed red peppers
1 clove garlic, minced	3 Tbsps. wine vinegar
1 tsp. grated ginger root	½ cup soy sauce
or ¼ tsp. powdered ginger	2 Tbsps. dark molasses
½ tsp. saffron powder	½ cup hot water
½ cup ground Brazil nuts	

Trim fat and remove as much connective tissue and membrane as possible from lamb cubes. Cover with wine vinegar in non-metal container and marinate for several hours.

Work all ingredients for seasoning paste together till smooth. If it is too thick, add a little vinegar from the marinade. Rub well into lamb cubes, brush lightly with oil and let stand at room temperature for 1 hour.

DIPPING SAUCE: Blend garlic, ground peanuts and crushed red peppers with vinegar. Add soy sauce, molasses and hot water and simmer gently for 15 minutes in an enamel or stainless steel saucepan.

On a well-oiled grill over hot coals, broil lamb 5 or 6 minutes, brushing frequently with oil and turning to brown evenly.

Serve immediately with community or individual dunking bowls of the dipping sauce.

SKEWERED LAMB WITH SWEETBREADS AND TOMATOES

1 *lb. meat from leg of baby lamb, cut into 1-inch cubes*
1 *pair veal sweetbreads (about 1 lb.)*
4 *Tbsps. melted butter*
½ *tsp. paprika*
16 *cherry tomatoes*

Marinade for lamb:
½ *cup olive oil*
¼ *cup lemon juice*
¼ *cup finely chopped parsley*
1 *tsp. salt*
½ *tsp. black pepper*

Trim fat and remove as much connective tissue and membrane as possible from lamb cubes.

SWEETBREADS: To prepare sweetbreads for use, see pages 117-118, and then cut into 1-inch cubes, cover and refrigerate until ready to broil.

Combine marinade ingredients and pour over lamb cubes. Marinate for an hour or more.

Brush sweetbread pieces generously with melted butter and sprinkle with paprika. Skewer lamb, alternating with tomatoes and sweetbreads.

Grill over medium high charcoal bed for 7 or 8 minutes, turning skewers to brown meat evenly and brushing with melted butter.

UNADORNED LAMB CHOPS, CHARCOAL-GRILLED

8 loin or rib lamb chops,
   single-cut

4 Tbsps. melted butter
salt and pepper to taste

Trim excess fat from chops. Brush with a little melted butter.

Grill over hot coals for 2 or 3 minutes on each side. Remove to platter. Brush with a little melted butter, add a sprinkle of salt and a twist of the pepper mill.

Serves 4.

CHARCOAL LAMB CHOPS WITH FRESH MINT

4 loin lamb chops, 1 inch
   thick
¼ cup lemon juice
¼ cup chopped fresh mint
   leaves
 or 1¾ Tbsps. dried mint
   leaves

1 tsp. grated lemon rind
¼ tsp. sugar
½ tsp. salt
⅓ cup olive oil

Trim fat from lamb chops and make several slits around edges.

Pour lemon juice into bowl of blender. Add mint leaves, lemon rind, sugar and salt. Blend at high speed for 5 seconds. Pour into bowl and mix well with olive oil.

Place chops on a china or glass platter and pour mint mixture over them, turning to coat thoroughly. Let stand for at least an hour at room temperature to season, turning occasionally.

Remove chops from mint sauce and grill over medium hot coals for 7 or 8 minutes on each side, basting with sauce.

STUFFED LAMB CHOPS, GRILLED

4 *double loin lamb chops*
½ *tsp. black pepper*
3 *Tbsps. melted butter*

Stuffing:
2 *whole chicken livers*
2 *Tbsps. sweet butter*
3 *shallots, minced*
4 *large mushrooms, minced*
1 *Tbsp. parsley, snipped fine*

1 *slice lean raw bacon,*
  minced
¼ *tsp. salt*
2 *oz. dry vermouth*
1 *egg yolk, slightly beaten*
1 *Tbsp. cognac*

Have butcher make a pocket in each double chop by cutting from the bone toward the center. Trim fat around edges.

To MAKE STUFFING: Sauté chicken livers in butter. When they have cooked through, break them into pieces with a fork. To same skillet add chopped shallots, mushrooms, parsley, minced bacon and salt. Sauté until vegetables are soft. Add vermouth and simmer slowly for several minutes. Remove from heat and cool. Blend in beaten egg yolk to bind and add tablespoon of cognac.

Fill pockets of chops with stuffing and secure with small pin-type skewers. Sprinkle chops with a little black pepper, brush with butter and grill over medium hot coals. Place a loose tent of foil over chops while cooking. Grill 8 minutes on first side, turn, brush with butter, and grill 6 to 8 minutes on second side.

TRANSYLVANIAN LAMB STEAKS
WITH PAPRIKA AND GARLIC

2 lbs. lamb steak, cut ½ inch
    thick from leg and
    pounded slightly
1 Tbsp. salt
2 cloves garlic

2 Tbsps. lemon juice
1 Tbsp. sweet paprika
6 medium onions, sliced
4 lemons, sliced very thin,
    with skin

Mash salt and garlic in small bowl. Add lemon juice and paprika. Rub paste into trimmed lamb steaks.

Place a layer of onion and lemon slices in bottom of a non-metal container wide enough to accommodate 1 steak laid out flat. Cover with seasoned steak, then another layer of onions and lemon and top with remaining meat. Final layer should be the lemon and onion slices. Press down with wooden spoon. Cover and refrigerate overnight. Remove to room temperature at least 1 hour before grilling.

Grill meat on oiled grid over hot coals for 5 minutes on each side. Don't worry if a few onion or lemon slices cling to the meat. It only improves the flavor.

Serves 4.

GRILLED LAMB STEAKS WITH GINGER
AND LIME

2 lbs. lamb steak, cut ½ inch
    thick from leg and
    pounded slightly
½ tsp. salt
¼ cup olive oil

4 Tbsps. lime juice
1 Tbsp. grated lime rind
1 Tbsp. grated fresh ginger
    root
    or ½ tsp. powdered ginger

Trim fat from lamb steaks and season lightly with salt.

Combine olive oil, lime juice, lime rind and ginger and pour over steaks on a glass or china platter. Turn to coat evenly. Marinate 1 hour at room temperature.

Drain steaks and grill over hot coals 5 minutes on each side, basting with marinade several times.

Serves 4.

CURRIED LAMB MEATBALLS
(SKILLET)

2 *lbs. ground lamb*
¼ *cup dried currants*
1 *medium onion, minced*
3 *Tbsps. butter*
1 *tsp. salt*
¼ *tsp. ground cumin*
¼ *tsp. ground coriander*
¼ *tsp. ground turmeric*

¼ *cup ground toasted
   almonds*
2 *Tbsps. minced parsley*
2 *Tbsps. lime juice*
½ *cup yoghurt*
2 *eggs, slightly beaten*
2 *Tbsps. peanut oil*

Cover currants with boiling water and let soften for ½ hour. Sauté onion in 1 tablespoon butter. Add salt, cumin, coriander, turmeric, and combine with lamb, drained currants, almonds and parsley. Add lime juice, yoghurt and beaten eggs. Mix lightly but well, and shape into small balls. Chill for several hours. Remove from the refrigerator ½ hour before ready to cook.

In a heavy skillet over a hot bed of coals, heat 2 tablespoons butter and the peanut oil. Sauté the meatballs 6 to 8 minutes, turning to brown evenly. Don't crowd the pan. As they are done, remove them with a slotted spoon to a warm platter.

These meatballs are excellent served plain or with a curry sauce (see page 105) which can be made ahead of time and reheated when ready to serve.

CURRY SAUCE

4 Tbsps. butter	¼ tsp. powdered ginger
1 Tbsp. flour	½ tsp. salt
1 cup finely chopped onions	¼ tsp. white pepper
1 tart apple, peeled and	1½ cups chicken stock
chopped	¼ cup grated coconut
2 Tbsps. Indian curry powder	½ cup coconut milk*
¼ tsp. mace	½ cup heavy cream

Combine 1 tablespoon softened butter with 1 tablespoon flour. Set aside.

Sauté onions and apple in 3 tablespoons butter until soft but not browned. Stir in curry powder, mace, ginger, salt and white pepper. Pour in chicken stock and simmer gently for 10 minutes. Add butter-flour mixture in small bits, stirring to blend well.

Add grated coconut, coconut milk and heavy cream. Correct seasoning and heat gently for 5 minutes. Do not boil.

If you make this sauce ahead of time, reheat it very slowly over a low flame. Never allow it to boil.

*TO MAKE COCONUT MILK FROM FRESH COCONUT: Crack open the coconut, discard the fluid, remove white meat from the shell and cut into small chunks. For ½ cup coconut meat use 1 cup hot milk. Put a small amount of hot milk in the blender, add coconut, blend for 30 seconds. Add the rest of the milk, blend until smooth. Let stand for ½ hour and then strain.

TO MAKE COCONUT MILK FROM PACKAGED COCONUT: Add 1 cup hot milk to ½ cup shredded coconut. Let stand for ½ hour and then strain.

This curry sauce is equally good with lamb, seafood or chicken.

INDIAN LAMB PATTIES

2 lbs. lean ground lamb
3 Tbsps. lime juice
1 tsp. salt
1 Tbsp. crushed coriander
   seeds

1 tsp. powdered saffron
¼ cup cashew nuts
¼ cup yoghurt
2 Tbsps. olive oil

Put lime juice, salt, coriander seeds and saffron in bowl of blender. Blend for a few seconds, then add cashews and yoghurt and blend until mixture is smooth.

Blend yoghurt mixture with lamb. Mix lightly but thoroughly and form into 8 patties. Chill.

When ready to cook, remove lamb patties from refrigerator, brush them with olive oil and place in well-oiled handgrill. Remove grid from top of hibachi and grill over hot coals, turning only once, for 3 or 4 minutes on each side.

NEAR EAST LAMBURGERS

2 lbs. lean lamb, ground
1 onion, grated fine
2 egg yolks, slightly beaten
2 Tbsps. fresh parsley,
   chopped fine
1 Tbsp. fresh mint, chopped
   fine

¼ cup pignolia nuts, coarsely
   chopped
1 tsp. salt
½ tsp. white pepper
2 Tbsps. ice water
3 Tbsps. olive oil

Combine the ground lamb and grated onion. Stir in beaten egg yolks. Add parsley, mint, pignolia nuts, salt and pepper.

Add 2 tablespoons ice water and knead mixture until it is smooth. Apply small amount of olive oil to hands and form mixture into 8 patties. Chill.

When ready to cook, brush patties with olive oil and place on well-oiled hand-grill. Remove grid from hibachi. Grill over hot coals, turning only once, for 3 or 4 minutes on each side.

LAMBURGERS STUFFED WITH FRUIT AND NUTS

2 lbs. ground lamb
1 medium-size onion, grated
1 tsp. salt
½ tsp. rosemary
1 Tbsp. grated lemon rind
4 Tbsps. yoghurt

6 cooked apricot halves
6 tsps. chopped toasted
    almonds
6 slices lean bacon, cooked
    slightly

Combine ground lamb and grated onion. Season with salt and rosemary. Add grated lemon rind and yoghurt. Mix thoroughly. Form into 12 patties, 6 of which should be thicker than the other 6.

Press 1 drained apricot half into each of the 6 thick patties. Sprinkle 1 teaspoon chopped toasted almonds into cavity of each apricot. Top with thinner patty. Press edges together. Wrap precooked bacon slice around each patty and secure with toothpick. Chill until ready to grill.

Place in oiled hand-grill over medium hot coals on hibachi with grid removed. Grill 7 minutes on each side.

HAM KEBABS WITH SPICED CRABAPPLES

2-lb. ham steak, cut 1 inch
    thick (ready-to-eat
    ham)
1 jar spiced crabapples (10
    or 12 apples)

syrup from crabapples
2 Tbsps. lemon juice
1 Tbsp. grated lemon rind
½ tsp. mustard powder
4 Tbsps. honey

Trim excess fat from meat and cut into 1-inch cubes. Skewer ham and crabapples, alternating about 2 cubes of ham with 1 apple.

Combine syrup from crabapples with lemon juice, lemon rind, mustard and honey.

Raise hibachi grill to highest level from hot coals. Grill

ham kebabs for 10 minutes, turning to brown evenly. Remove skewers from grill and brush on glaze generously. Return to grill and broil, turning occasionally, until glaze is browned, about 4 or 5 minutes.

GRILLED HAM STEAK

1 *ham steak, center slice, cut 1½-inch thick (from ready-to-eat ham)*

Glaze:
4 *Tbsps. honey*   1 *Tbsp. grated horseradish*
2 *Tbsps. melted butter*   1 *tsp. Worcestershire sauce*

Trim most of fat from ham. Cut shallow gashes around edges, every 2 or 3 inches, to keep ham from curling.
Combine glaze ingredients.
Raise hibachi grill to highest level from medium bed of hot coals. Broil ham for 8 minutes on each side. Remove steak to platter, completely cover both sides with glaze and return to grill. Broil an additional 2 minutes on each side, or until glaze is browned.
Serve steak cut in serving-size pieces, or carve in thin slices, across the grain.

Glaze Variations:
3 *Tbsps. light molasses*   1 *tsp. dry mustard powder*
2 *Tbsps. soy sauce*   2 *Tbsps. lemon juice*

Combine ingredients.

2 *Tbsps. butter*   1 *Tbsp. Worcestershire sauce*
1 *onion, grated*   2 *Tbsps. brown sugar*
3 *Tbsps. catsup*   ½ *cup dry red wine*

Sauté onions in butter for 5 minutes, add remaining ingredients and simmer an additional 5 minutes.

GRILLED HAM CUBES WITH BANANAS, FIGS AND PORT WINE

2-*lb. steak from ready-to-eat*
   ham, 1 *inch thick*
3 *bananas, just ripe*
2 *Tbsps. lemon juice*
1 *medium can Kadota figs,*
   drained

Port Sauce:
½ *cup port wine*
1 *small onion, grated*
juice from figs
4 *Tbsps. orange juice*
¼ *cup beef bouillon*
1 *Tbsp. grated orange rind*
¼ *tsp. ground allspice*

SAUCE: Combine ingredients and simmer over low flame for 15 minutes.

Trim excess fat from ham and cut into 1-inch cubes. Peel bananas and slice into 1-inch pieces. Sprinkle banana slices with lemon juice. Skewer ham cubes alternately with bananas and figs. Lay skewers on platter and cover with sauce, turning to coat evenly.

Raise hibachi grill to highest level from hot coals. Grill kebabs 12 to 15 minutes in all, turning and brushing with wine sauce.

BARBECUED PORK CHOPS

4 *center loin pork chops, cut*
   1 *inch thick*
½ *cup red wine vinegar*
1½ *cups water*
1 *clove garlic, minced*

½ *tsp. salt*
4 *Tbsps. Worcestershire*
   sauce
2 *or* 3 *drops Tabasco sauce*

Trim all the fat from chops and place in a glass or china dish with vinegar, water, garlic and salt. Refrigerate for 24 hours, turning 3 or 4 times.

Remove chops from marinade and dry them thoroughly

with paper towels. Brush each side well with combined Worcestershire and Tabasco.

Adjust well-oiled grill of hibachi to second level over a hot bed of coals. Grill 12 to 15 minutes on each side, turning only once. Brush several times during grilling with Worcestershire mixture.

PORK WITH VEGETABLES AND PEANUTS
(SKILLET)

1½ lbs. lean pork	2 Tbsps. sherry
3 Tbsps. peanut oil	2 Tbsps. oyster sauce
¾ cup shelled peanuts	(available in Oriental
1 clove garlic, pressed	food shops)
1 leek, sliced thin	1 Tbsp. cornstarch
2 stalks celery, diced fine	½ cup beef consommé
½ cup mushrooms, sliced	¼ cup water chestnuts, sliced
thin	thin
2 Tbsps. soy sauce	3 scallions, chopped fine

Trim fat from pork and simmer slowly in enough water to cover for 30 minutes. Drain, cool thoroughly and slice into thin strips, cutting across the grain.

In heavy skillet, over high bed of coals, heat 1 tablespoon peanut oil. Sauté peanuts until golden, stirring to prevent burning. With slotted spoon, remove to absorbent paper to drain.

Pour remaining oil in skillet. When it is hot, add garlic, stir, then add leek, celery and mushrooms. Stirring constantly, cook for 3 minutes. Stir in soy sauce, sherry and oyster sauce. Add pork slices and cook for 2 or 3 minutes. Add combined cornstarch and consommé, cook 2 additional minutes to thicken. Stir in water chestnuts and sautéed peanuts. Heat thoroughly, stirring to prevent sticking since mixture will be thick.

Serve at once, sprinkled with finely chopped scallions.

BARBECUED SPARERIBS

4 to 5 lbs. lean spareribs
½ cup toasted almonds,
    slivered

Marinade:
1 cup soy sauce
1½ tsps. black pepper
4 Tbsps. grated orange rind
1½ tsps. mustard powder
1 garlic clove, pressed

Basting and Serving Sauce:
2 cups beef bouillon
2 Tbsps. brown sugar
1 tsp. MSG or Accent
2 cups orange juice
¼ cup vinegar
1 Tbsp. cornstarch
1½ cups chopped onions
1 cup chopped green peppers
1 jar preserved kumquats,
    in syrup

Have butcher saw through spareribs horizontally, cutting them in half. Cut these into 2- or 3-rib serving portions.

Combine marinade ingredients, coat ribs well, and let stand for 3 or 4 hours, turning occasionally.

Meanwhile, make sauce: In large saucepan, heat beef bouillon. Add brown sugar, MSG, orange juice and vinegar. Stir in cornstarch, dissolved in 2 or 3 tablespoons of water. Simmer, stirring, for 5 minutes. Add onions, green peppers, chopped kumquats and their juice. Simmer slowly for 20 minutes. Sauce is now ready.

Drain marinade from ribs, reserving liquid, and place ribs on a rack in a roasting pan in a 450° oven (preheated) for 15 to 20 minutes. This is to remove some of the fat. Turn ribs once during this period, brushing on some of the marinade to keep them moist. After 20 minutes, turn oven down to 325°. Remove roasting pan from oven, lay ribs on paper towels to absorb fat, pour off fat from pan and remove rack.

Combine any remaining marinade with toasted almonds and orange sauce. Pour some of this sauce into bottom of roasting pan, cover with layer of ribs and more sauce over all. Cover roasting pan and bake in 325° oven for 1 hour.

Spareribs may now be safely charcoal-grilled on the hibachi.

Note: Everything up to this point can be done ahead of time, even the day before. If it is done this early, cool ribs in sauce and store, covered, in refrigerator. Remove to room temperature at least an hour before ready to grill.

Just before ready to grill, lift ribs from sauce onto platter. Heat sauce and bring spareribs and hot sauce to the hibachi for the final and most important step.

On a well-oiled grill over medium hot coals, grill ribs for about 15 minutes in all. To prevent drying out, turn and baste often with sauce. The crusty charcoal flavor of spareribs prepared this way is very special.

GRILLED PORK CHOPS WITH HERBS

4 loin pork chops, cut 1 inch thick	¼ tsp. ground sage
	¼ tsp. ground juniper berries
1½ cups papaya juice	¼ tsp. freshly ground black
1 tsp. salt	pepper
¼ tsp. allspice	4 Tbsps. butter, melted

Trim all the fat from chops and marinate covered, in a glass or china dish, in the papaya juice for 24 hours. Turn and baste 3 or 4 times.

Combine salt, allspice, sage, juniper berries and pepper with 1 tablespoon of the papaya juice marinade to make a thick paste.

Drain chops and dry them thoroughly with paper towels. Rub seasoning paste into the surface of the meat. Brush with melted butter.

Adjust grill of hibachi to highest level over a high bed of coals. During grilling, cover top of chops loosely with a foil tent. Lift foil to baste with butter several times while cooking. Grill 12 to 15 minutes on each side, lowering level of grill as coals burn down. Pork chops should be cooked thoroughly.

Kidneys

Lamb or veal kidneys are recommended because their flavor is delicate. Trimmed of outer fat casing, lamb kidneys weigh between 1½ to 2 ounces each; veal kidneys, from 6 to 8 ounces.

Kidneys are more tender and juicy when cooked very quickly over intense heat; therefore, the hibachi is an ideal method.

Preparation:
1. Trim excess fat and remove outer membrane.
2. Cut the kidney in half lengthwise.
3. With a small, sharp-pointed knife or curved manicure scissors, remove hard white center core.
4. Rinse in cold water and dry with paper towels.

GRILLED LAMB KIDNEYS WITH MUSHROOMS AND TOMATOES

6 *prepared lamb kidneys*
12 *mushroom caps*
2 *Tbsps. butter*
12 *cherry tomatoes*

Marinade:
½ *cup dry vermouth*
¼ *cup olive oil*
1 *small onion, grated*
1 *Tbsp. prepared mustard*
1 *tsp. salt*
2 *Tbsps. parsley, chopped fine*

Cut prepared lamb kidneys (see above) into 1½-inch pieces. Let stand at room temperature for 1 hour in combined marinade ingredients.

Wash and, if necessary, peel mushroom caps. Sauté gently in butter for 5 minutes.

Alternate kidney pieces on skewers with mushrooms and

cherry tomatoes. Grill over hot coals 5 or 6 minutes at most, turning to brown evenly and brushing frequently with marinade.

KIDNEY SLICES WITH SHALLOTS AND MUSHROOMS
(SKILLET)

3 *veal kidneys*	1 *cup fresh mushrooms,*
salt to taste	*sliced thin*
½ *tsp. pepper*	1 *tsp. dried tarragon*
4 *Tbsps. butter*	1 *tsp. Worcestershire sauce*
2 *Tbsps. olive oil*	½ *cup dry white wine*
6 *shallots, sliced thin*	3 *Tbsps. parsley, chopped*
	fine

Cut properly prepared kidneys (see page 113) across into thin (⅛-inch) slices. Season with salt and pepper.

In heavy skillet, over high bed of hot coals, heat 2 tablespoons butter and 2 tablespoons olive oil. When good and hot add kidney slices. Do not overcrowd pan. Sauté quickly, less than a minute on each side. As they are cooked, remove kidney slices to heated platter.

Add remaining 2 tablespoons of butter to skillet, and sauté shallots and mushrooms for 3 minutes. Stir in tarragon, Worcestershire sauce and wine. Simmer for 3 or 4 minutes, stirring to prevent sticking or burning. Return kidney slices to pan, heat through.

Stir in chopped parsley and serve at once.

GRILLED CALVES' LIVER

1½ lbs. calves' liver, in
   1-inch slices (have
   butcher remove skin
   and tubes)
2 Tbsps. lemon juice
1 tsp. MSG or Accent
3 oz. sweet butter

1 Tbsp. finely chopped
   parsley
1 Tbsp. finely chopped chives
1 Tbsp. finely chopped basil
   (if dry herbs are used, use
   1 tsp. each)
salt and pepper

Wipe liver slices with a damp cloth, sprinkle with lemon juice and MSG. Let stand for 15 minutes.

Melt butter and add parsley, chives and basil. Brush on liver slices.

On oiled grid over medium hot bed of coals, grill liver for 6 minutes on first side. Baste with butter, turn, baste, and grill an additional 6 minutes. Test to see if properly done. Overcooking will make liver leathery. It should be pink inside to be tender. Add salt and pepper to taste.

GRILLED CALVES' LIVER CUBES WITH ONIONS AND BACON

1 lb. calves' liver, in 1-inch
   slices
½ tsp. MSG or Accent
½ lb. Canadian bacon,
   ¼-inch slices

12 small white onions
3 oz. melted butter
1 tsp. paprika
½ tsp. salt

Trim tubes and skin from liver. Cut into 1-inch cubes. Sprinkle with MSG. Cut bacon into 1-inch squares.

Parboil onions for 10 minutes. Drain and peel.

Thread liver, bacon and onions alternately on skewers. Brush with melted butter.

Grill over medium hot coals for a total of 10 minutes, brushing with butter, and turning to brown evenly.

Serve with sprinkling of paprika and salt and the remaining butter. Liver should be pink inside and crusty on the outside.

CALVES' LIVER STRIPS, ORIENTAL STYLE
(SKILLET)

1 *lb. calves' liver*
½ *tsp. MSG or Accent*
½ *tsp. black pepper*
1 *small green pepper*
1 *Tbsp. cornstarch*
4 *Tbsps. peanut oil*
1 *tsp. sesame oil (optional)*
2 *scallions, sliced fine*
½ *cup pineapple chunks,*
    drained (reserve juice)
¼ *cup toasted almonds,*
    chopped

Marinade:
2 *Tbsps. soy sauce*
½ *clove garlic, pressed*
¼ *tsp. crushed red peppers*
1 *Tbsp. grated fresh ginger*
    root
or ½ *tsp. powdered ginger*
½ *cup pineapple juice, plus*
    juice from drained
    chunks
¼ *cup dry sherry*

Have liver sliced as thin as possible, no more than ¼ inch thick. Cut slices into 1-inch strips. Sprinkle with MSG and pepper. Let stand in combined marinade ingredients for ½ hour or more. Drain, reserving marinade.

Wash, seed and cut green pepper lengthwise into thin strips. Parboil for 3 minutes. Drain and dry.

Make a thin paste of 1 tablespoon cornstarch and a little of the marinade. Gradually add rest of marinade to cornstarch paste and stir until smooth.

In heavy skillet over high bed of glowing coals, heat 3 tablespoons of peanut oil. When very hot, add liver strips and brown quickly on both sides. When they no longer bleed when pricked with fork, remove strips to a heated platter.

Add remaining peanut oil and sesame oil and when hot, sauté scallions and green pepper strips for 2 minutes, stirring. Stir marinade-cornstarch mixture (cornstarch will settle to bottom when it stands) and add to scallions and green peppers in pan. Simmer, stirring constantly, until clear and slightly thickened. Return sautéed liver strips with pineapple chunks, simmer for 1 minute, or until heated through. Sprinkle with chopped almonds, stir through once and serve immediately.

CALVES' LIVER, ITALIAN STYLE
(SKILLET)

1 *lb. calves' liver, sliced very thin*
4 *Tbsps. olive oil*
1 *large onion, sliced paper thin*
1 *tsp. oregano*
salt and pepper
2 *Tbsps. minced parsley*
lemon wedges

Cut liver slices into 2 or 3 pieces.

Heat 2 tablespoons olive oil in heavy skillet over hot bed of glowing charcoal. Sauté onion slices, stirring, for 3 or 4 minutes. Push onion to one side of pan, add remaining olive oil and oregano. When oil is good and hot, add liver, brown very quickly, cooking no more than a minute on each side. Sprinkle with salt and pepper, mix in the onion. Cook 1 additional minute, sprinkle with chopped parsley.

Serve with lemon wedges.

Sweetbreads

A sweetbread consists of 2 connecting parts, and has a thin membrane and connective tissue. The sweetbread of a calf weighs approximately 1 pound. With proper preparation, it is a delicacy and can be most successfully hibachi-cooked.

CAUTION: Sweetbreads are highly perishable. They should be bought at a reputable shop and used the day of purchase.

Preparation:

1. Wash thoroughly under running cold water.
2. Place in a pan of ice water for 1 hour. Drain.
3. Put sweetbreads in an enamel or stainless steel saucepan, cover by 2 inches with cold water containing 3 table-spoons lemon juice and 1 teaspoon salt. Bring slowly to a boil and barely simmer, uncovered, for 15 minutes. Drain.
4. Plunge sweetbreads in ice water (with 6 ice cubes) and leave for 15 minutes. Drain.
5. Remove membrane and trim any ragged or discolored portions.
6. Sweetbreads are now ready to use.

SWEETBREAD AND SAUSAGE KEBABS
WITH STUFFED PRUNES

1 *whole veal sweetbread*   2 *Tbsps. grated orange rind*
   (*about 1 lb.*)   1 *Tbsp. honey*
12 *small link pork sausages*   2 *oz. butter, melted*
12 *large tenderized prunes*   *salt and pepper*
3 *Tbsps. ground peanuts*

Soften prunes by covering with boiling water. Let stand for several hours. Drain. Carefully remove pits and fill centers with a combination of ground peanuts, grated orange rind and honey.

Precook sausages for 15 minutes by simmering in skillet with ½ cup of water. Drain sausages on absorbent paper.

Cut prepared sweetbreads (see above) into 1½-inch squares. Dip into melted butter and season lightly with salt and pepper.

Thread sweetbread squares, stuffed prunes and sausages alternately on long skewers, taking care not to crowd them.

On well-oiled grid over medium bed of glowing coals, grill for a total of 6 to 8 minutes, turning to brown evenly, and basting with melted butter. Do not overcook.

MEAT · 119

GRILLED HERBED SWEETBREADS WITH CAPERS

2 small veal sweetbreads
2 Tbsps. lemon juice
salt and pepper
¼ lb. butter

2 Tbsps. chives, chopped fine
2 Tbsps. capers, mashed
½ tsp. rosemary

Split each half of prepared (see page 118) and chilled sweet-bread lengthwise into 2 pieces. Sprinkle with lemon juice and season lightly with salt and pepper.

Melt butter and add chives, capers and rosemary.

Dip sweetbread pieces into melted herb butter and place on well-oiled hand-grill.

Remove grid of hibachi and place hand-grill directly over medium bed of coals. Broil 4 minutes, brush with butter, turn and grill second side an additional 4 or 5 minutes. Baste top with butter during final grilling.

Serve at once with remaining heated butter.

WIENERS AND SAUERKRAUT

8 fat wieners
8 slices lean bacon
¼ lb. sauerkraut

1 tart apple, grated
½ tsp. caraway seeds
8 frankfurter rolls

Pan-fry bacon for 3 minutes to remove excess fat. Remove from pan while still limp and drain.

Simmer sauerkraut with grated apple and caraway seeds over low heat for 10 minutes.

Split wieners, lengthwise, to within ¼ inch of the other side. Fill with sauerkraut mixture. Wrap bacon slice in spiral around wiener, securing at each end with a small pin-type skewer or toothpick.

Grill over medium hot coals, turning, for 10 to 12 minutes. Serve on toasted frankfurter rolls.

SPECIAL GRILLING SAUCE
(for Meat or Chicken)

¼ cup olive oil	½ tsp. powdered mustard
2 anchovy fillets	½ tsp. ground chili peppers
1 clove garlic	½ bay leaf, crumbled
¼ cup chopped parsley	½ tsp. salt
½ cup chopped onions	1 Tbsp. brown sugar
½ cup sliced mushrooms	½ cup water
1 cup dry red wine	

Pour 2 tablespoons olive oil into blender bowl. Add anchovy fillets, garlic and parsley. Blend until smooth. Gradually add chopped onions and mushrooms and blend until it is a purée.

Scrape contents of blender into a heavy, deep saucepan (with lid) and stir in remaining olive oil, red wine, mustard, ground peppers, bay leaf, salt, brown sugar. Mix well, add water, and simmer slowly for 45 minutes, stirring occasionally to prevent sticking.

Cool and store in a tightly closed jar in refrigerator. This sauce will keep for weeks.

Just before grilling, brush this sauce on steak, hamburger, pork chops, veal or chicken, and use it for basting.

FOWL

Fowl

The tenderest young chicken or duckling requires more broiling time than fish, seafood or tender cuts of meat. Nothing in the world is less palatable than a piece of chicken charred black on the outside and still raw inside. This is the result of grilling too short a time with "too much heat too soon."

However, you can have juicy, tender, properly cooked fowl, with the added advantages of charcoal flavor and aroma, if you will follow a few simple rules when using your hibachi for this kind of cooking:

1. Since fowl takes longer to broil, build a bed of coals sufficiently high to burn at least an hour. Start your hibachi 1 hour before you plan to grill, and place the briquettes 3 to 4 layers deep. Be sure the briquettes have burned to glowing coals before starting to grill.

2. For direct grilling, adjust the hibachi grill to the highest level away from the coals.

3. Fowl requires frequent basting to keep it from becoming dry. Turn pieces often, changing position so that the heat hits from all angles.

4. Remember: Anything with sugar or soy tends to char quickly, so use such a sauce or glaze during the last 5 to 10 minutes of grilling, when the fowl is almost cooked.

5. When pieces of chicken or duck are wrapped in individual foil packages, the liquids are sealed in. Turn packages carefully to avoid puncturing, otherwise juices will escape. The foil can be opened up or removed to crisp and brown the fowl during the last 5 to 10 minutes of grilling. When foil wrapping is used, start grilling at first or second level above the coals.

6. To prepare duckling for hibachi grilling, trim all visible fat and partially cook by simmering or roasting to remove as much fat as possible. This will cut down on charring and smoking due to flare-ups when melting fat hits the hot coals.

7. By partially cooking chicken ahead of time, grilling time can be reduced considerably.

8. Marinades containing wine, vinegar, lemon juice or lime juice help to tenderize the flesh of fowl. Be sure to marinate in a non-metal container.

9. Excessive dryness and charring of fowl can be reduced by covering the surface of the grill with foil. Cut foil large enough so that you can turn up edges all around to form a shallow retaining wall for the basting juices. Remove foil during last 5 to 10 minutes and broil on uncovered grill directly over coals for final browning and crisping.

10. For individual packages or for covering the grill top, the flavor and smoke of the charcoal will penetrate the food if you wad the foil up in a loose ball, then smooth it out. (If you hold the smoothed-out sheet up to the light you will see pinpoints of light.)

11. For many Oriental dishes requiring quick stir-cooking over high heat, remember that raw fowl cooks in a few minutes if it is diced fine or sliced thin or shredded.

BARBECUED CHICKEN

3 *lb. broiler-fryer, cut into* 8 *pieces*

Marinade:
¼ *cup olive oil*	½ *tsp. salt*
¼ *cup lime or lemon juice*	3 *drops Tabasco sauce*
1 *tsp. grated lime rind*	1 *small onion, grated*
½ *clove pressed garlic*	¼ *tsp. black pepper*
1 *tsp. chili powder*	3 *Tbsps. catsup*

Mix marinade ingredients well and pour over chicken pieces, in non-metal bowl. Cover and refrigerate for 2 to 3 hours, turning pieces occasionally. Remove bowl to room temperature ½ hour before grilling.

Oil hibachi grill and adjust to highest level over high bed of glowing coals. Drain excess marinade from chicken pieces and place them on grill. Baste often with marinade and turn frequently to brown evenly. Grill until tender and thoroughly cooked. This will take from 30 to 45 minutes, depending on size and tenderness of chicken and variation in bed of coals. As coals burn down, adjust grill to lower level.

CHICKEN WITH HERBS

2 *plump broilers, cut into pieces (use backs and wings for another dish)*

Seasoning Paste:	Marinade:
¼ lb. butter	1 *cup dry white wine*
2 *Tbsps. chopped chives*	½ *cup olive oil*
2 *Tbsps. chopped watercress (optional)*	1 *lemon, juice and grated rind*
2 *Tbsps. chopped fresh parsley*	3 *dashes Angostura bitters*
or 1½ *tsp. dried parsley*	
1 *Tbsp. chopped fresh tarragon*	
or 1½ *tsp. dried tarragon*	
1 *tsp. powdered marjoram*	

Soften butter at room temperature and blend in chives, watercress, parsley and tarragon. (Use fresh herbs if possible.) Add marjoram. With small, sharp-pointed knife, gently lift skin of chicken and insert as much herb butter as possible between skin and flesh. Reserve any remaining herb butter.

Combine marinade ingredients, pour over chicken pieces in a deep non-metal bowl and marinate in refrigerator, covered, overnight. Remove to room temperature 1 hour before grilling.

Cut squares of double duty foil large enough to wrap individual servings of chicken completely. Dot inside of foil with small bits of herb butter, lay chicken piece on butter, fold up edges of foil, ladle a tablespoonful of marinade over chicken piece, seal package by folding edges of foil over and down.

Adjust grill to second level over deep bed of glowing coals. Grill for 35 to 40 minutes, turning often and carefully. Lower level of grill. Transfer foil packages to platter, remove foil, drain juice from packets into small bowl. Return unwrapped chicken to grill for an additional 10 to 12 minutes, basting with juices in bowl and turning to brown evenly.

GRILLED MARJORAM CHICKEN

2 2-lb. broilers, quartered
1 tsp. salt
freshly ground pepper
1 onion, grated fine

juice of 2 lemons
2 Tbsps. powdered marjoram
¼ lb. butter

Wipe chicken with damp cloth. Remove any bones which will pull out easily. Season with salt and pepper to taste and let stand for 10 minutes.

Sprinkle grated onion and lemon juice over chicken. With fingers, briskly rub powdered marjoram on chicken. Pieces should be brownish in color.

Melt butter and dip each chicken piece to coat well.

Cut a sheet of heavy duty foil large enough to cover top of grill. Wad it into a ball and smooth it out again (see general hints on grilling fowl). Adjust grill to highest level over a high bed of glowing coals. Cover with foil, and grill chicken for 20 minutes on each side. Baste frequently with melted butter. As coals burn down, adjust grill to lower level.

If additional browning is desired, remove foil, baste chicken with butter, and return to grill, turning to brown evenly.

BROILED CHICKEN WITH PLUM AND CHUTNEY SAUCE

2 2-lb. broilers, cut into pieces (use backs and wings for another dish)

Sauce:

1 cup plum preserves
½ cup prepared chutney
    (Major Grey's)

3 Tbsps. lime juice
2 Tbsps. brown sugar
3 Tbsps. butter

To MAKE SAUCE: Combine plum preserves, chutney, lime juice and brown sugar in blender bowl. Cover and blend at high speed until smooth. Transfer to saucepan and simmer, with butter, over low heat for 10 minutes.

Dip each chicken piece in sauce and wrap individually in a square of foil large enough to fold up and seal in an envelope package.

Grill over high bed of glowing coals (with grill adjusted to second height from coals) for 40 minutes, turning packets to cook all sides. As coals burn down, adjust grill to first level. Remove chicken from foil, brush with additional sauce, and glaze directly over coals for 2 or 3 minutes on each side.

Heat remaining sauce and serve with chicken.

GRILLED CHICKEN INDIENNE

2 2-lb. broilers, cut into pieces
    (use backs and wings for
    another dish)
6 Tbsps. butter
1 medium-size onion, grated
juice of 2 lemons
1 Tbsp. toasted sesame seeds
1 tsp. turmeric

1 tsp. poppy seeds
1 tsp. crushed dry red pepper
1 tsp. coriander
1 tsp. cumin
1 tsp. chopped mint leaves
½ tsp. powdered ginger
1 tsp. salt

To make seasoning paste, put butter, grated onion, lemon juice and all the seeds and spices into the blender. Blend until it is a thick smooth paste. (Mixture can be crushed and pounded into paste with a mortar and pestle.)

With a small, sharp-pointed knife, carefully raise skin from chicken pieces. With your fingers, rub the seasoning paste between the skin and the flesh of the chicken. Be generous! Press skin back into place and rub the outside of each piece with the seasoning paste.

Wrap each piece of chicken in foil, folding to make seal tight. Place any remaining seasoning paste in small bowl and bring to hibachi on tray with chicken packets.

Over hot coals, with grill adjusted to medium height, grill chicken for 30 minutes. Turn pieces over and around often, but carefully, so as not to puncture foil. As coals burn down, adjust grill to lower level. After 30 minutes, remove packets from grill to platter. As you open each package, pour juice from package into bowl with remaining seasoning paste. Discard foil. Dip chicken pieces in sauce in bowl and return to grill, basting and turning, to crisp. Grill until tender.

SPICY CHINESE CHICKEN
(SKILLET)

3 *whole chicken breasts (broilers)*
4 *scallions*
3 *Tbsps. dry sherry*
3 *Tbsps. water*
1½ *Tbsps. cornstarch*
8 *dried Chinese mushrooms or ¼ lb. fresh mushrooms*
12 *water chestnuts*
1 *small can bamboo shoots*
4 *Tbsps. peanut oil*
3 *slices fresh ginger root or 1 tsp. powdered ginger*
3 *Tbsps. soy jam (hoisin sauce)*
1 *cup nut meats (cashews, almonds, walnuts or pecans)*

Remove chicken meat from bones and cut into ¼-inch cubes. Cut scallions (with green) into ½-inch diagonal slices.

Mix sherry and water with cornstarch. Mix well with

chicken cubes and scallion slices and leave in refrigerator at least an hour.

Pour boiling water over mushrooms to cover, if dried Chinese variety is used, and allow to stand for 20 minutes. Slice mushrooms thin. Dice water chestnuts. Slice bamboo shoots into thin strips. Set up tray with ingredients conveniently and attractively laid out: bowl with marinated chicken and scallions, separate dishes for water chestnuts, bamboo shoots, mushrooms, peanut oil, garlic press for use with ginger root slices, soy jam (hoisin), nuts.

Have firebox well built up with hot coals.

Heat peanut oil in a large heavy skillet until smoking hot. Using garlic press, squeeze ginger root into oil, add chicken and scallion mixture and stir constantly for 2 minutes or until chicken turns white. Add bamboo shoots, water chestnuts and mushroom slices. Continue stirring for another 2 minutes. Add soy jam (hoisin), stirring to heat and mix well. Just before serving, stir in the nut meats. Serve with white rice.

Serves 6.

Note: Chinese mushrooms, fresh ginger root and soy jam or hoisin sauce are available in most Oriental food shops and can be obtained by mail. The hoisin sauce comes in one-pound cans but can be stored in a closed jar in refrigerator for months. Water chestnuts and bamboo shoots are in most large supermarkets.

JAPANESE BROILED CHICKEN
(Yakitori)

2 *whole chicken breasts*	Sauce:
6 *scallions*	½ *cup shoyu or soy sauce*
cayenne pepper	½ *cup sake (rice wine)*
	or *sherry or vermouth*
	2 *Tbsps. brown sugar*
	1 *tsp. pressed fresh ginger*
	root
	or ½ *tsp. powdered ginger*

Split, skin and bone chicken breasts and cut into ¾-inch squares. Clean scallions and cut into ¾-inch lengths.

On well-soaked long bamboo skewers, alternate chicken and scallion pieces.

Combine shoyu, wine, brown sugar and ginger and pour over skewered chicken and scallions in a deep platter. Marinate at least 1 hour, turning occasionally.

Set oiled grill at level highest from glowing charcoal bed. Lift skewers from marinade and drain excess. Grill for 10 to 12 minutes, removing from heat 3 or 4 times to roll in marinade.

Remove from coals, sprinkle lightly with a little cayenne pepper. If desired, marinade can be used as a dip.

Note: Chicken livers, cut into pieces the size of the chicken squares, can be marinated and alternated on the skewers with the chicken and scallions.

CHICKEN KEBABS WITH CHERRIES AND MUSHROOMS

3 *whole chicken breasts from small plump broilers*
16 *small fresh mushrooms* or *canned mushroom caps*
2 *Tbsps. butter*
1 *can pitted Bing cherries, in syrup*

Marinade:
½ cup syrup, drained from cherries
¼ cup dry red wine
4 Tbsps. lemon juice
2 Tbsps. peanut oil
1 Tbsp. sesame oil (optional)
3 Tbsps. finely chopped chives
    or 1 small onion, grated
½ tsp. each salt and pepper
1 tsp. dry mustard
¼ tsp. grated nutmeg

Split, skin and bone chicken breasts. Cut into ¾ to 1-inch squares.

Combine marinade ingredients and mix thoroughly. Pour over chicken and marinate for at least 1 hour.

Wash, stem and, if necessary, peel mushrooms. Sauté mushroom caps in 2 tablespoons butter for 5 minutes.

On well-soaked long bamboo or thin metal skewers alternate chicken cubes with mushroom caps and cherries. Do not place too close together. Brush generously with marinade.

Set oiled grill at level highest from glowing charcoal bed. Grill kebabs for 10 to 12 minutes, until chicken is tender but not dried out. Baste and turn frequently.

If desired, marinade can be used as a dip.

CHICKEN WITH MACADAMIA NUTS AND SNOW PEAS
(SKILLET)

2 *whole chicken breasts from broilers (about 1½ lbs.)*
1 *12-oz. can clear chicken consommé*
½ *lb. fresh mushrooms*
3 *scallions*
1 *small can water chestnuts*
½ *lb. fresh snow peas*
or 1 *box frozen snow peas*

1 *small can sliced bamboo shoots*
4 *Tbsps. peanut oil*
½ *tsp. salt*
½ *tsp. white pepper*
1 *Tbsp. cornstarch*
¼ *cup coarsely chopped Macadamia nuts*

Simmer chicken breasts for 10 minutes in chicken consommé. Reserve broth. Skin, bone and slice chicken diagonally into thin slivers.

Clean and trim mushrooms. Peel, if necessary, and slice thin. Slice scallions diagonally into ⅛-inch pieces. Drain water chestnuts and slice thin. If snow peas are fresh, trim and string. Drain bamboo slices.

Heat peanut oil in heavy skillet over high coal-bed. Sauté scallions and mushrooms, stirring constantly, for 2 minutes. Add chicken. Season with salt and pepper and stir-fry 2 minutes. Add water chestnuts and bamboo shoots and stir. Add reserved chicken broth to which you have added cornstarch. Cook, stirring, and add snow peas. Simmer until mixture is smooth and thickened. Stir in chopped Macadamia nuts and serve at once.

INDONESIAN SKEWERED CHICKEN
(Saté Ajam)

2 *whole breasts from plump broilers (about 1½ lbs.)*
3 *oz. melted butter*

Marinade:
1 *onion, grated*
1 *garlic clove, pressed*
1 *tsp. salt*
½ *tsp. powdered cumin*
¼ *cup mild vinegar*
¼ *cup water*

Serving Sauce:
1 *cup beef bouillon*
2 *medium onions, quartered*
1 *clove garlic, peeled and halved*
1 *Tbsp. tamarind pulp*
  or 2 *Tbsps. lime or lemon juice*
¼ *tsp. crushed red peppers*
½ *cup ground Indonesian almonds*
  or *ground cashews, walnuts, peanuts or almonds*
2 *Tbsps. peanut oil*
2 *Tbsps. dark molasses*
1 *tsp. salt*
2 *Tbsps. soy sauce*

Bone and skin chicken breasts. Cut into ¾-inch squares.

Combine onion, garlic, salt, cumin, vinegar and water and pour over chicken pieces in non-metal container. Let stand for 1 hour.

FOR SERVING SAUCE: Pour ¼ cup of the bouillon into blender bowl. Add onions, garlic, tamarind pulp or lemon or lime juice, red peppers and nuts. Blend until smooth. Heat peanut oil in skillet. Scrape contents from blender into skillet and sauté for 5 minutes. Add molasses, salt, soy sauce and remainder of bouillon. Stir and simmer gently for 10 minutes.

Skewer chicken pieces and brush with melted butter.

Adjust oiled grill to second level over medium hot bed of coals. Grill skewered chicken, turning often and basting with melted butter, for about 15 minutes, or until tender.

Serve with heated serving sauce.

SURPRISE CHICKEN ROLLS

2 *whole breasts from plump broilers (split and boned)*
salt
white pepper
6 *whole chicken livers, cut in quarters*
6 *Tbsps. butter*

4 *shallots minced fine or 1 small onion, minced*
6 *medium-size mushrooms, chopped fine*
2 *Tbsps. sour cream*
8 *thin slices of prosciutto or boiled ham*
1 *tsp. paprika*
3 *Tbsps. Parmesan cheese*

Remove skin from chicken and divide each half of chicken breast into two slices. Place each slice between 2 pieces of waxed paper and pound until thin. Season to taste.

Sauté chicken livers in 3 tablespoons butter for 5 minutes. Remove chicken livers to small chopping bowl, and sauté minced shallots and mushrooms in same pan. Chop livers, or mash with a fork. Add sautéed shallots and mushrooms to bowl, season with salt and pepper to taste, and mix thoroughly. Add sour cream to make spreading consistency.

On each slice of chicken lay a slice of ham. Place 2 teaspoons liver mixture in center of ham slice. Make a neat roll, tucking in ends to make a secure packet. If necessary, skewer with toothpicks or tie with heavy thread.

Melt remaining 3 tablespoons of butter, stir in paprika, and dip each roll to coat well with butter. Wrap each roll in foil. Grill over medium coals for 15 to 20 minutes. Transfer to platter and remove foil.

Brush with additional melted butter and sprinkle lightly with Parmesan cheese. Return to grill for 5 minutes, to melt and brown cheese. Turn once.

CHICKEN SUKIYAKI
(STIR-FRY)

The recipe for chicken sukiyaki is basically the same as that given for beef sukiyaki (see page 79).

The only variations are:

For	Substitute
beef	*2 whole chicken breasts, skinned, boned and partially frozen, then sliced across the grain into paper-thin strips*
beef suet	*chicken fat*
beef bouillon	*good strong chicken broth*

DUCK SUKIYAKI

Substitute thin slivers of raw duck.
Use chicken fat and chicken broth for duck sukiyaki.

SKEWERED CHICKEN LIVERS WITH MUSHROOM CAPS AND ARTICHOKE HEARTS

1½ *lbs. fresh chicken livers*
1 *tsp. salt*
½ *tsp. pepper*
3 *Tbsps. flour*
12 *medium-size mushrooms (caps only)*

6 *Tbsps. melted butter*
12 *artichoke hearts (canned) in olive oil*

Rinse, dry and halve chicken livers. Sprinkle with salt and pepper and dust lightly with flour.

Sauté mushroom caps for 4 or 5 minutes in 1 tablespoon of butter. Drain artichoke hearts.

Skewer chicken liver halves alternately with mushroom caps and artichoke hearts on long thin skewers.

On oiled grid over medium hot coals, grill for 7 or 8 minutes, turning and basting with butter.

SHERRIED CHICKEN LIVERS
(SKILLET)

1½ lbs. chicken livers
1 tsp. salt
½ tsp. pepper
3 Tbsps. flour
4 slices bacon
3 scallions, including green
    tops, chopped fine
½ cup beef consommé

¼ cup sherry
¼ cup chopped ripe black
    olives
1 small can pimientos,
    cut in narrow strips
2 Tbsps. finely chopped
    parsley

Cut chicken livers into quarters. Season with salt and pepper and dust lightly with 2 tablespoons of flour.

Pan-fry bacon until crisp. Drain on absorbent paper. Reserve 3 tablespoons of bacon fat. Crumble bacon into small bits.

Heat 1 tablespoon of bacon fat in heavy skillet over high bed of glowing coals. Sauté chopped scallions for 2 minutes. Push to one side of skillet. Add 2 more tablespoons of bacon fat, and when it is hot, brown chicken livers quickly. Remove to heated platter when done.

Pour half of beef consommé into skillet and scrape pan to loosen brown bits. Mix 1 teaspoon flour with remaining consommé and add to pan. Stir for 1 minute, then add sherry, olives and pimientos. Heat, stirring, for 1 or 2 minutes, then return livers and crumbled bacon to pan. When mixture is bubbling hot, sprinkle with chopped parsley and serve at once.

CHICKEN LIVERS AND MUSHROOMS
WITH PISTACHIO NUTS
(SKILLET)

1 *lb. chicken livers*	1 *tsp. salt*
½ *lb. mushrooms*	1 *cup strained chicken broth*
3 *Tbsps. butter*	1 *Tbsp. arrowroot*
2 *Tbsps. olive oil*	½ *cup chopped pistachio nuts*
2 *Tbsps. chives, chopped fine*	1 *Tbsp. chopped parsley*
¼ *tsp. thyme*	*pepper, freshly ground*
¼ *tsp. sage*	

Rinse, dry and cut chicken livers into quarters. Wash mushrooms (peel if necessary), and slice into thin strips.

Heat 2 tablespoons of butter and 1 tablespoon of olive oil in heavy skillet over high bed of glowing charcoal. Brown chicken livers quickly, and remove to warm platter when they do not bleed if pricked with a fork.

Add remaining butter and oil and when hot, add sliced mushrooms. Sauté, stirring, for 3 or 4 minutes, sprinkle with chives, thyme and sage, and mix. Add chicken broth, well blended with arrowroot. Simmer, stirring, until clear and slightly thickened. Return sautéed chicken livers to skillet, add pistachio nuts, and stir to combine all ingredients. When bubbling hot, sprinkle with salt, parsley and a generous twist of pepper mill. Serve at once.

GRILLED CORNISH HENS

2 *Cornish hens*	½ *tsp. paprika*
juice of 1 *lemon*	4 *Tbsps. olive oil*
½ *tsp. salt*	2-3 *oz. grated Swiss or*
½ *tsp. pepper*	*Parmesan cheese*

Completely thaw frozen Cornish hens. Split in half. Remove any bones or cartilage which will pull out easily.

Sprinkle hens with lemon juice, and season inside and out with salt, pepper and paprika. Brush with olive oil.

Cover grill with wadded, then smoothed-out foil (see page 123) and adjust to highest level over high bed of glowing coals. Lay Cornish hen halves, skin side down, on foil. Grill for 10 minutes, brushing frequently with olive oil. Turn and grill other side, basting, for 12 minutes or until cooked through. Lower grill to first level.

Transfer hens to platter, brush with oil and sprinkle each side with grated cheese. Remove foil from grill and return hens to direct charcoal heat for 2 to 3 minutes on each side to melt and brown cheese.

Serves 2.

DUCKLING WITH VEGETABLES AND NUTS
(SKILLET)

1 4 *to* 5-*lb. duckling*

Marinade:
1 *Tbsp. cornstarch*
2 *Tbsps. soy sauce*
¼ *cup dry sherry*
1 *Tbsp. honey*
1 *tsp. fresh ginger root,*
    pressed
or ¼ *tsp. ground ginger*
½ *tsp. pepper*

Broth:
duck carcass and giblets
2 *stalks chopped celery*
1 *onion, sliced*
2 *cups chicken consommé*
½ *cup orange juice*
3 *Tbsps. grated orange rind*
½ *tsp. salt*
½ *tsp. pepper*
¼ *tsp. cinnamon*

For Final Step:
combined broth and marinade
1 *cup shredded carrots*
1 *cup finely sliced*
    mushrooms
¼ *cup finely chopped*
    scallions

½ *cup blanched fresh bean*
    sprouts
or *rinsed canned sprouts*
6 *Tbsps. peanut oil*
½ *cup chopped pecans*
2 *oz. orange liqueur*
2 *Tbsps. chopped chives*

FISH AND SEAFOOD

Fish and Seafood

It is not possible to give a complete list of all edible fish, but any fish which can be broiled can be charcoal-grilled.

Names of fish will differ from one region to another and fish available in one area are not always marketed in other parts of the country. However, many of the recipes given in this section are interchangeable. For example, a porgy can be substituted for a butterfish or one type of small fillet for another.

If you follow a few simple rules and suggestions, hibachi-cooked fish is delicious:

Fish *must* be fresh. If you're not lucky enough to have a fisherman in the family, buy from a reliable fish dealer. Frozen fish should be used as soon as possible after thawing. Never refreeze it.

Don't use too hot a fire. Fish has a more delicate flesh than meat or fowl and must be grilled over a lower bed of coals or with grill adjusted to a greater distance from more intense heat.

Don't overcook fish. It will become dry and tasteless.

Use an oiled hand-grill (flat toaster-type or basket-grill) to facilitate handling and turning of fish. Remove the grid from top of hibachi and place hand-grill directly over coals.

Baste often. Fish is very lean and should be brushed liberally and frequently with oil or butter while grilling.

A wrapping of wet corn husks or leaves will keep fish fillets and steaks juicy yet allow the charcoal flavor to penetrate.

A wrapping of heavy aluminum foil will seal in the seasoning and juices.

Fish are marketed as follows:

WHOLE FISH: as they come from the water

DRAWN FISH: whole fish with viscera removed

DRESSED FISH: whole fish, scaled, with viscera removed, head, tail and fins removed

STEAKS: cross-section slices from large dressed fish

FILLETS: sides of the fish, cut lengthwise away from the backbone (they vary from ¼ to 1 inch in thickness and in weight according to type and size of fish)

SHELLFISH (includes clams, oysters, mussels, scallops, shrimp, crab, lobsters):

Fresh shellfish is highly perishable and must never be eaten unless absolutely fresh.

Clams, oysters and mussels should have tightly closed shells.

Scallops should be firm and white.

Shrimps should be greenish-gray in color and firm to the touch.

Crab meat is available, cooked and chilled, in lump or flake form.

Once again the advice: buy from a reliable fish dealer.

Frozen shellfish should be used as soon as possible after thawing. Never refreeze.

BLUEFISH, SPLIT AND GRILLED

1 4 to 5-lb. bluefish, cleaned,   ½ tsp. salt
    scaled, head removed,   ½ tsp. paprika
    and split for broiling   1 Tbsp. chopped chives
husks from 4 ears of corn   1 Tbsp. chopped parsley
6 Tbsps. melted butter

Drop corn husks in boiling water to cover. Simmer 10 minutes. Drain and spread a layer of husks on lower side of hand-grill.

Brush skin of bluefish halves with melted butter and lay, skin side down, on corn husks. Sprinkle salt, paprika, chopped chives and parsley on top of fish. Brush generously with melted butter. Cover with scant layer of corn husks.

Remove grid from hibachi. Place hand-grill directly over medium bed of glowing coals, with flesh side toward coals. Grill 8 minutes, turn, and grill 10 minutes on skin side.

Remove to serving platter, brush with remaining heated butter and serve immediately.

GRILLED BUTTERFISH

4 small butterfish, drawn,   ½ tsp. freshly grated nutmeg
    with heads and tails   2 Tbsps. lemon juice
    intact   4 Tbsps. olive oil
1 tsp. salt   2 Tbsps. grated lemon rind
1 tsp. black pepper

Cut several diagonal slits on each side of cleaned butterfish.

Make a thick seasoning paste by combining salt, pepper, nutmeg, 1 tablespoon lemon juice and 1 tablespoon olive oil, adding a little additional oil if necessary. Rub inside of fish with seasoning paste and insert small bits of paste into diagonal slits. Add grated lemon rind and 1 tablespoon lemon juice to remaining olive oil. Brush on fish, place in hand-grill.

Remove grid from hibachi and put hand-grill directly over

medium bed of glowing coals. Grill 4 minutes on each side, basting with oil as you turn. Test to see if done.

GRILLED YELLOWTAIL FLOUNDER

1½ lbs. fillets of yellowtail   ½ tsp. paprika
    flounder   4 Tbsps. melted butter
juice of 1 lemon   ½ Tbsp. "fish herbs" *

Wipe fillets with damp cloth and sprinkle with lemon juice and paprika.

Combine melted butter and fish herbs. Dip each fillet in butter and place on hand-grill.

Remove grid from hibachi and grill directly over medium coals for 2 or 3 minutes on each side. Fish is done when it flakes easily. Baste several times with herb butter while grilling.

* See page 158.

FLUKE FILLETS GRILLED IN CORN HUSKS WITH HAZELNUT STUFFING

4 small fluke, filleted   Stuffing:
husks from 4 ears of corn   ¼ cup finely chopped onions
2 Tbsps. lemon juice   2 Tbsps. butter
½ tsp. salt   1 pimiento, sliced fine
¼ tsp. pepper   3 Tbsps. black olives,
4 Tbsps. melted butter   chopped
lemon wedges   ½ tsp. sweet paprika
                                               ¼ cup finely chopped
                                                  hazelnuts

Drop corn husks into boiling water to cover. Simmer 10 minutes. Drain and set aside.

Sauté chopped onions in butter until soft. Add pimiento

and chopped olives. Sprinkle with paprika and stir in chopped hazelnuts. Remove from fire.

Combine lemon juice, salt and pepper with 4 tablespoons melted butter.

Spread a layer of drained corn husks on lower surface of a hand-grill. Dip one of the fillets into the seasoned lemon butter, lay it on the corn husks. Spread hazelnut stuffing to within ½ inch of the edges of the fillet, dip a second fillet into lemon butter and lay it on the first fillet. Press edges together. Repeat with pairs of remaining fillets and stuffing. Cover the top of the stuffed fillets with another layer of drained corn husks. Close hand-grill.

Grill over medium bed of hot coals 7 minutes on each side, turning once. Serve with remaining lemon butter and lemon wedges.

Note: Any thin fillets are good this way. If they are thicker, increase grilling time accordingly.

HALIBUT STEAKS CREOLE

2 halibut steaks, approximately 1 lb. each, ¾ inch thick

Creole Sauce (to be made in advance):

1 *cup onions, chopped fine*	⅛ *tsp. cayenne pepper*
⅓ *cup green peppers, chopped fine*	2 *Tbsps. butter*
	2 *Tbsps. olive oil*
1 *celery stalk and leaves, chopped*	1 *cup stewed tomatoes (fresh or canned)*
1 *tsp. salt*	¼ *cup tomato purée*
½ *tsp. black pepper*	¼ *cup water*
¼ *tsp. garlic powder*	4 *Tbsps. brown sugar*
¼ *tsp. basil*	4 *Tbsps. lemon juice*
	½ *bay leaf, crumbled*

SAUCE: Sauté onions, peppers, celery, with salt, pepper,

garlic powder, basil and cayenne, in butter and olive oil. After 10 minutes, add tomatoes, tomato purée, water, brown sugar, lemon juice and bay leaf. Mix thoroughly, cover, and simmer slowly for 1 hour. Stir occasionally to prevent scorching. Add a little water if it becomes too thick. Reserve until ready for use.

Cut 2 pieces of heavy foil large enough to cover the 2 steaks when stacked together. Put one piece of foil on top of the other to form a double layer. Pour a generous portion of the Creole sauce on the foil, turning up the edges slightly so that sauce will not run off. Lay one of the steaks on the sauce, cover this steak with sauce and top with second piece of fish. Ladle sauce over the top. Fold up foil and seal securely.

Place halibut on grill over medium bed of glowing coals. Grill for 12 minutes on each side, turning carefully to avoid puncturing foil. Fish should flake easily when tested.

Remove to serving platter. Pour remaining heated Creole sauce over all.

SMOKED KIPPERS

2 smoked kippers	2 Tbsps. grated onion
4 Tbsps. melted butter	2 Tbsps. lemon juice

Open kipper out flat and brush generously with combined butter, grated onion and lemon juice. Close kipper and place on oiled hand-grill.

Remove grid from hibachi and place hand-grill directly over medium bed of glowing coals. Grill for 5 minutes on each side.

If you like the flesh part browned a little more, open kipper up and grill, flesh side down, an additional minute.

Note: Try these charcoaled kippers with new potatoes boiled in their jackets, or with scrambled eggs.

GRILLED SPANISH MACKEREL

1 3-lb. mackerel, cleaned and
    split for broiling
½ tsp. salt
¼ cup melted butter
2 Tbsps. lemon juice

1 Tbsp. Bahamian mustard
    or 1 tsp. brown mustard
    mixed with ½ tsp. pre-
    pared horseradish and
    pinch of brown sugar
¼ cup thinly sliced green
    olives

Wipe mackerel with damp cloth. Sprinkle flesh with salt. Combine butter with lemon juice and mustard, brush skin side lightly, flesh side liberally. Place on oiled hand-grill.

Remove grid from hibachi and put hand-grill directly over medium bed of glowing coals. Grill mackerel, flesh side toward coals, for 5 or 6 minutes. Turn, brush with butter, and grill an additional 5 minutes, or until flesh flakes easily. Remove to hot platter.

Heat remaining butter with sliced green olives and pour over mackerel. Serve at once.

STRIPED SEA MULLET
WITH BAY LEAVES

2 striped mullet (1½ to 2
    lbs. each), split, cleaned
    and head removed
4 Tbsps. melted butter
2 Tbsps. lemon juice
2 Tbsps. finely chopped
    parsley

½ tsp. savory
½ tsp. salt
½ tsp. paprika
1 generous handful dried bay
    leaves (about ¾ cup)

Combine melted butter with lemon juice, parsley and savory. Sprinkle inside of fish with salt and paprika and brush generously with lemon butter. Brush skin side with lemon butter and place in a well-oiled hand-grill.

Remove grid from hibachi. Place hand-grill directly over medium bed of glowing coals. Grill for 5 minutes, flesh side toward coals, turn, brush with butter, and grill an additional 5 minutes on skin side. Remove hand-grill just long enough to sprinkle half the bay leaves directly onto the coals. Quickly return fish, flesh side down, for about half a minute to absorb some of the flavor of the burning bay leaves.

Remove fish to a fireproof platter and surround fish with remaining bay leaves. Light the bay leaves in several places and serve immediately. The visual effect is attractive and the additional aroma and flavor add to the enjoyment of the fish.

YELLOW PIKE WITH FRESH MINT

1 3 *to* 4-*lb. yellow pike*
  or 2 *smaller ones, split and*
    cleaned
juice and grated rind of
  1 *lemon*

salt
black pepper
4 *Tbsps. butter*
1 *Tbsp. chopped fresh mint*
  or 1 *tsp. dried mint leaves*

Remove head, tail and fins from fish. Sprinkle flesh with lemon juice, salt and pepper.

Combine softened butter with mint and lemon rind and rub on inside and outside of fish. Put the 2 halves of fish together and place fish on oiled foil. Fold foil up and seal securely with double fold.

Place wrapped fish on oiled grill over medium high bed of glowing coals. Grill 6 or 7 minutes on each side. If using smaller fish, cut grilling time to 5 minutes on each side. Test to see if done. Fish should flake easily. If not done satisfactorily, continue grilling in open package for another few minutes.

PORGIES WITH BACON AND MUSHROOMS

4 *small porgies* (*no more than ¾ lb. each*)
salt
8 *slices lean bacon, partially cooked*

¼ *cup sweet onion, chopped fine*
½ *cup thinly sliced mushrooms*
¼ *tsp. paprika*
¼ *tsp. black pepper*

Have porgies split, cleaned and heads removed. Wipe with damp cloth and sprinkle sparingly with salt.

To remove excess fat, partially cook bacon, removing to drain while it is still limp. Pour off all but 1 tablespoon of fat.

In the same skillet, sauté onions and mushrooms until soft. Season with paprika and pepper. Cool slightly and fill cavities of porgies. Wrap 2 slices of bacon around each fish, securing with toothpicks or small pin-type skewers. Lay prepared fish in hand-grill.

Remove grid from hibachi and place hand-grill directly over a medium bed of glowing coals. Grill for 5 or 6 minutes on each side, or until bacon is crisp and the fish flakes easily when tested.

ROCKFISH SHIOYAKI

Shioyaki (shio-"salt"—yaki-"broil") is a Japanese method of charcoal grilling in which salt is the all-important ingredient. Mackerel, red snapper, striped bass, salmon or any firm-fleshed fish can be broiled in this way.

2 *lbs. rockfish* (*weight after dressing*) *cut into ¾-inch slices*

2 *tsps. salt*
2 *lemons or limes*

Wipe fish with damp cloth. Depending on size of steaks and your grilling surface, skewer 2 or 3 small rockfish slices on 3 thin 10 to 12-inch skewers. (See illustration). Sprinkle half the salt over both sides of steaks. Place skewers on a platter and let stand at room temperature for 30 minutes.

Raise well-oiled grill of hibachi to highest level from medium bed of glowing coals. Sprinkle remaining salt on fish. Grill 4 minutes on first side. Grasp skewers at narrow end, turn, and grill 6 minutes on second side or until fish flakes easily when tested.

Serve sprinkled with lemon or lime juice.

Serves 4.

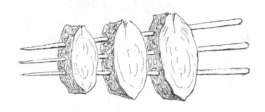

BROILED SALMON STEAKS WITH DILL SAUCE

2 *center-cut salmon steaks,*
    ¾ to 1 inch thick
1 *tsp. salt*
¼ *cup melted butter*
2 *Tbsps. lemon juice*

Sauce:
2 *eggs*
1 *cup sour cream*
⅓ *cup chopped fresh dill*
    or 2 Tbsps. dried dill weed
⅛ *tsp. cayenne pepper*
½ *tsp. white pepper*
salt

SAUCE: Beat eggs until foamy and yellow. Stir into sour cream with chopped dill, cayenne, pepper and salt to taste. Chill thoroughly.

Wipe salmon steaks with damp cloth. Sprinkle with salt and let stand at room temperature for 15 minutes to absorb salt. Combine melted butter and lemon juice. Brush both sides of salmon steak generously. Lay on oiled hand-grill.

Remove grid from hibachi and place hand-grill directly over medium bed of glowing coals. Grill salmon 4 or 5 minutes on one side, basting with lemon butter. Turn, baste, and grill 4 or 5 minutes on the other side. Do not overcook. Salmon flakes easily when done.

Remove salmon to heated platter. Serve at once with chilled dill sauce in a community or individual bowls.

GRILLED SCROD

Scrod is a young codfish; it is lean and tasty but tends to fall apart very easily. It is preferable, therefore, to grill it in crumpled, then smoothed-out foil which allows the charcoal flavor to permeate but prevents the fish from falling apart. (See page 123.)

2 lbs. scrod fillets   ½ tsp. paprika
2 Tbsps. lime juice   4 Tbsps. melted butter
1 tsp. salt

Wipe fillets with damp cloth. Sprinkle with lime juice, salt and paprika.

Brush fillets with melted butter. Lay each one flat on a piece of foil cut large enough to fold up into a package. Pour any remaining butter over fillets and seal each package with a double fold.

Place foil packets on grill over medium bed of coals. Grill 6 to 7 minutes on each side, turning once. Serve in foil.

SEA SQUAB
(SKILLET)

In the Middle Atlantic fishing area, this tasty seafood is known by many less attractive names such as blowfish, swellfish, puffer, toad or globefish. In recent years, the fishing industry refers to this fish as "sea squab" and markets only the tails, skinned and ready to cook. These vary in size anywhere from 2 to 10 tails to a pound.

1½ lbs. sea squab
1 tsp. salt

6 Tbsps. peanut oil
½ garlic clove, mashed

Chilled Sauce:
¼ cup pignolia nuts
2 hard-cooked egg yolks
1 tsp. prepared hot mustard
1 tsp. Worcestershire sauce
½ tsp. salt
1 tsp. capers

2 Tbsps. wine vinegar
¼ cup grated Parmesan
    cheese
½ cup mayonnaise
1 Tbsp. chopped chives

SAUCE: Combine pignolia nuts, hard-cooked egg yolks, mustard, Worcestershire, salt, capers and vinegar in blender bowl and blend at high speed until smooth. Add, with grated cheese, to mayonnaise and mix well. Sprinkle with chopped chives and chill in covered bowl until ready to use.

Wipe sea squab with a damp cloth and sprinkle with salt.

In a heavy skillet over high hot bed of glowing coals, heat peanut oil. Stir in mashed garlic, then quickly sauté sea squab 3 or 4 minutes on each side, turning carefully. Time will vary with size of tails, but flesh will flake easily when done. When properly cooked and browned, remove to heated plates and serve with chilled sauce.

GRILLED BONED SHAD

1 4 to 5-lb. shad, filleted and
    completely boned
2 Tbsps. lime or lemon juice

½ tsp. salt
¼ tsp. black pepper
3 Tbsps. butter (very cold)

Sprinkle boned shad with lime juice. Season with salt and pepper.

Cut ice-cold butter into small slivers and insert into pockets where bones have been removed.

Place fillets on oiled hand-grill. Remove grid from hibachi and place hand-grill over medium bed of hot coals. Broil for no more than 2 or 3 minutes on each side, brushing with a little melted butter before turning.

Serve as is—and immediately.

Note: The flavor of shad is so special it needs little seasoning.

GRILLED ANCHOVY-STUFFED SMELTS

16 *very small smelts*   ½ *cup mayonnaise*
8 *flat anchovy fillets*   1 *Tbsp. mustard powder*

Have fish dealer just draw smelts (which means he will leave head and tail intact and remove the viscera without splitting the fish). Wash drawn smelts in cold salted water and dry well with paper towels.

Insert half an anchovy fillet into each smelt into opening made where fish was drawn and close it with a small pin-type skewer or toothpick.

Combine mayonnaise and mustard and brush outside of each smelt. Place smelts in hinged hand-grill.

Remove grid from hibachi and place hand-grill directly over medium coals. Grill 2 or 3 minutes on first side, brush with additional mustard-mayonnaise, turn and grill 2 or 3 minutes on second side. Test to see if done.

GRILLED RED SNAPPER
STUFFED WITH SMOKED MUSSELS

3 to 4-lb. red snapper
½ tsp. paprika
2 Tbsps. lemon juice

1 Tbsp. chopped chives
4 Tbsps. melted butter
one 1½-oz. jar smoked
    mussels

Have fish drawn and cleaned, leaving on head and tail. Sprinkle with paprika, lemon juice and chives. Brush with melted butter, inside and out.

Drain mussels and place in cavity of fish. Close opening with small pin-type skewers. Place on oiled hand-grill.

Remove grid from hibachi and put hand-grill directly over medium bed of glowing coals. Grill for 8 minutes on first side, brush with butter, turn and grill second side 8 to 10 minutes, or until fish flakes easily. Do not overcook.

FILLET OF SOLE WITH FENNEL

1½ lbs. fillet of sole
1 tsp. salt
6 Tbsps. melted butter

Marinade:
⅓ cup lime juice, freshly
    squeezed
1½ tsps. fennel seeds
2 Tbsps. cognac

Pour lime juice into blender with fennel seeds. Blend at high speed until seeds are crushed. Combine with cognac for marinade.

Wipe fillets with damp cloth, sprinkle with salt. Cover with marinade in a glass or enamel dish and let stand for an hour. Drain fillets, reserving marinade. Brush with melted butter and put into oiled hand-grill.

Remove grid from hibachi and place hand-grill directly over medium bed of glowing coals. Grill for 2 or 3 minutes on each side, brushing with melted butter. Do not overcook.

Remove to serving platter and sprinkle with remaining marinade.

SOLE WITH WHITE GRAPES

1½ lbs. small sole fillets
2 Tbsps. lemon juice
½ tsp. salt
½ tsp. paprika

Sauce:
6 shallots, sliced thin
4 Tbsps. butter
1½ cups white seedless
    grapes
¾ cup dry white wine

Wipe fillets with damp cloth. Sprinkle with lemon juice and salt.

Sauté shallots in butter until soft. Add grapes, stemmed and halved, and white wine. Simmer slowly for 5 minutes. Remove from fire and cool slightly.

For each 2 fillets, cut 1 piece of heavy foil, large enough to make a packet. Spread some of the grape sauce on each piece of foil, lay a fillet on the sauce, cover fillet with more sauce, and top with second fillet. Pour a generous amount of sauce over all; sprinkle lightly with paprika. Fold up edges of foil and seal package securely.

Place on grill over medium bed of hot coals. Grill 6 or 7 minutes on each side.

Serve with remaining sauce, heated.

GRILLED LEMON SOLE WITH AVOCADO SAUCE

4 fillets of lemon sole
½ tsp. salt
¼ tsp. white pepper
juice of 1 lemon
4 Tbsps. melted butter

Avocado Sauce:
1 large ripe avocado
pulp and juice of 1 small
    onion, grated
3 Tbsps. lemon juice
1 Tbsp. chopped parsley
½ tsp. salt
½ tsp. chili powder
2 or 3 drops Tabasco sauce
¼ cup sour cream

SAUCE: Peel, pit and mash avocado. Blend in pulp and juice of grated onion, lemon juice and parsley; season with salt, chili powder and Tabasco. Mix with sour cream and chill.

Wipe fillets with damp cloth, sprinkle with salt, pepper and lemon juice and let stand for 10 minutes. Brush well with melted butter. Place in well-oiled hand-grill.

Remove grid from hibachi and place hand-grill directly over medium bed of glowing coals. Grill for 2 or 3 minutes on each side, brushing with melted butter. Fish will flake readily when done.

Serve with chilled avocado sauce.

STRIPED BASS TERIYAKI

1 4 to 5-lb. striped bass, dressed and cut into ¾-inch slices
1 tsp. Accent or MSG

Marinade:

½ cup soy sauce
½ cup sake or very dry
   sherry
1½ Tbsps. brown sugar

2 tsps. fresh ginger, minced
   fine
   or ½ tsp. powdered ginger
2 scallions, chopped fine
1 Tbsp. lemon juice

Wipe fish slices with damp cloth, sprinkle with Accent, and place in a glass or pottery bowl.

Combine marinade ingredients, pour over fish and marinate for 1 hour, turning several times.

Remove striped bass from marinade and skewer, 2 or 3 slices to each set of 3 thin 10 or 12-inch skewers as in Shioyaki. (See page 151.) Raise well-oiled grill of hibachi to highest level from medium bed of glowing coals. Broil 4 minutes on first side, brush with marinade, turn, and grill an additional 6 minutes. Brush on marinade at least once more. Fish should flake easily when done. Fish can also be done in hand-grill.

Serve with remaining marinade as sauce.

SWORDFISH STEAK WITH LIME AND HERBS

1 swordfish steak, 4 to 5 lbs., about 2 inches thick

Marinade:
¼ *cup olive oil*
¼ *cup lime juice*
2 *tsps. "fish herb" seasoning**
salt and pepper to taste

Herb Butter Sauce:
¼ *lb. melted butter*
1 *Tbsp. "fish herb"*
seasoning

Combine marinade ingredients and brush very generously on both sides of swordfish steak. Refrigerate in non-metal container for several hours, turning several times to marinate evenly. Remove to room temperature at least ½ hour before grilling. Drain, adding remaining marinade to the combined melted butter and "fish herb" seasoning.

At grilling time, brush both sides of steak with butter sauce and place in a well-oiled flat basket-grill over hot bed of coals. Grill 12 to 15 minutes on each side, basting top side occasionally with melted butter sauce to keep fish juicy. Test by inserting sharp knife in thickest part of steak; when done meat should be white and firm.

Carefully remove swordfish to large platter, pour over remaining heated butter sauce and slice diagonally into serving-size pieces.

Will serve 6 to 8.

*"Fish herb" seasoning is put out by several spice packagers (Twin Trees, John Wagner and others). If unavailable, it can be approximated by combining equal amounts of sweet basil, thyme, fennel, marjoram, sage and parsley.

SWORDFISH KEBABS

2 lbs. swordfish steak,
    at least 1 inch thick
¼ cup lemon juice
2 tsps. oregano

1 tsp. salt
½ cup olive oil
12 large pimiento-stuffed
    green olives

Trim and cut steak into 1½-inch squares. Combine lemon juice, oregano and salt. Rub into swordfish squares and let them stand for ½ hour at room temperature to absorb seasoning. Dip fish squares into olive oil to coat, and skewer, alternating with olives.

On oiled grill over medium high bed of glowing coals grill kebabs, brushing frequently with olive oil, and turning to brown all sides. Grill 8 to 10 minutes. Test to see if done. Swordfish tends to become too dry with overcooking.

BROOK TROUT OVER CHARCOAL

4 small trout (approximately
    1 lb. each)
1 lemon, cut into small
    slivers (with skin)
2 Tbsps. lemon juice

salt
black pepper
6 Tbsps. melted butter
2 Tbsps. flour
4 lemon wedges

Have fish drawn and scaled, leaving head and tail intact. Cut 3 shallow diagonal slashes in the skin on each side of trout to prevent fish from curling when grilled. Insert sliver of lemon, with rind, into each slash.

Sprinkle inside and outside of each trout with lemon juice, a little salt and pepper and brush with melted butter. Dust skin with flour and lay fish in well-oiled basket-grill.

Remove grid from hibachi and place basket-grill directly over medium bed of glowing coals. Broil for 5 minutes on each side.

Serve with melted butter and lemon wedges.

TROUT WITH SHRIMP STUFFING

4 small trout
12 medium-size shrimp,
    boiled, shelled and
    deveined

1 egg yolk
1 Tbsp. heavy cream
1 Tbsp. chopped parsley
1 Tbsp. chopped chives
salt to taste

Prepare trout as in Brook Trout over Charcoal (page 159). Place remaining ingredients in blender and blend until smooth. Stuff shrimp mixture into opening of trout and close with pin-type skewers. Grill 6 minutes on each side.

CRAB MEAT WITH MACADAMIA NUTS
(SKILLET)

1 lb. lump crab meat
    (preferably fresh)
2 Tbsps. butter
2 Tbsps. olive oil
½ cup thinly sliced
    mushrooms
3 Tbsps. shallots, sliced thin
½ cup clam juice
½ tsp. salt

¼ tsp. pepper
½ cup heavy cream
2 egg yolks, slightly beaten
½ cup Macadamia nuts,
    coarsely chopped and
    toasted
1 Tbsp. finely chopped
    parsley

Carefully pick over crab meat to remove any shell particles or pieces of cartilage.

Over a high bed of glowing coals, heat butter and olive oil in a heavy skillet. Add thinly sliced mushrooms and shallots and sauté for about 5 minutes. Stir in clam juice and cook 2 minutes. Add crab meat and season mixture with salt and pepper. Heat for 2 or 3 minutes. Gently stir in heavy cream to which the egg yolks have been added and heat thoroughly. Try not to break up crab meat pieces when stirring. When mixture is hot, but not boiling, stir in toasted Macadamia nuts.

Sprinkle with parsley and serve at once.

SUBGUM FRIED RICE WITH CRAB MEAT
(SKILLET)

½ cup crab meat, cleaned carefully	6 water chestnuts, sliced thin
4 Tbsps. peanut oil	1 egg, beaten
½ cup thinly sliced mushrooms	3 cups cold boiled rice
	2 Tbsps. soy sauce
½ green pepper, parboiled, cut into thin strips	¼ cup slivered toasted almonds
	4 scallions, chopped fine

In heavy skillet over high bed of glowing coals, heat half the peanut oil. Add sliced mushrooms, green pepper strips and water chestnuts. Cook 2 or 3 minutes, stirring. Push vegetables to one side of skillet.

Stir in crab meat and cook 2 minutes. Pour beaten egg over crab meat and stir until cooked egg is in shreds. Push egg-crab meat mixture aside with vegetables, add remaining peanut oil to skillet and stir in cold cooked rice. Stir with a wooden spoon to prevent sticking or burning and to separate grains of rice. After 3 minutes, mix rice with crab meat and vegetables, adding soy sauce. Stir until heated through, add toasted almonds.

Serve at once, sprinkled with finely chopped scallions.

Note: Slivers of cooked chicken, shrimp, ham, lobster, pork or duck can be substituted for the crab meat. Other vegetables can be substituted or added.

LOBSTER AND NOODLES WITH
FRESH TOMATOES
(SKILLET)

1½ lbs. lobster meat, raw,
   from frozen lobster tails
   or meat from a freshly
   split uncooked lobster
4 oz. thin egg noodles
4 large ripe tomatoes, peeled
   and diced
6 scallions, including greens,
   cut diagonally into thin
   slices
¼ lb. fresh mushrooms,
   sliced thin
2 inner stalks celery, sliced
   diagonally into thin
   strips

½ cup fresh bean sprouts,
   blanched, and cut into
   2-inch pieces
   or canned bean sprouts
¼ cup sliced bamboo shoots
1 Tbsp. cornstarch
3 Tbsps. cold water
2 Tbsp. soy sauce
½ tsp. sesame oil (optional)
1 tsp. sugar
1 cup chicken broth
4 Tbsps. peanut oil

Partially thaw lobster tails. Slit down center of soft under-shell and remove lobster meat. Cut it across into ¼-inch slices, then cut slices in half.

Boil egg noodles *al dente*, rinse and drain. Place on tray with diced tomatoes and other vegetables prepared as directed. Mix cornstarch in a bowl with cold water until smooth, adding soy sauce, sesame oil and sugar, and add to tray. Heat chicken broth and bring in with tray.

In large heavy skillet over high hot bed of glowing coals, heat peanut oil. Put in lobster pieces when oil is hot and sauté, turning and stirring, for 1 minute. It need cook no longer! Add scallions, mushrooms and celery and cook, stirring for 2 or 3 minutes. Add tomatoes and stir for 2 more minutes. Stir in bamboo shoots and bean sprouts, adding warm chicken broth and cooked noodles. Stir in cornstarch-soy mixture and cook until slightly thickened and heated through.

Serve *hot!*

GRILLED LOBSTER TAILS WITH AVOCADO

4 medium-size lobster tails
   (about ½ lb. each),
   completely thawed
juice of 1 lime
½ tsp. salt
1 large ripe avocado

1 tsp. grated lime rind
2-3 dashes Tabasco sauce
2-3 dashes Angostura bitters
¼ tsp. garlic powder
2 Tbsps. chili sauce

Slit down center of undershell of lobster tails and remove soft part of shell with sharp knife or scissors. Bend tail section back enough to break shell joints so that lobster tail will not curl up during grilling. Sprinkle exposed lobster meat with lime juice and salt.

Peel, pit and mash avocado into smooth paste. Add grated lime rind, Tabasco, bitters, garlic powder and chili sauce. Spread a thin layer of avocado paste on lobster meat.

Over a medium bed of glowing coals, place lobster tails, shell side up, on well-oiled grill. Broil for 3 minutes, turn and brush on remaining avocado paste. Grill an additional 8 to 10 minutes.

GRILLED DEVILED LOBSTERS

2 chicken lobsters (1 to 1½ lbs. each)
lemon wedges

Devil Spread:
1 small can smoked oysters
¼ lb. butter
2 Tbsps. lemon juice
2 Tbsps. chopped chives

½ tsp. mustard powder
2-3 dashes Tabasco sauce
1 Tbsp. Worcestershire sauce

Have lobsters split lengthwise and cleaned. Crack claws and bend tail section back enough to break shell joints so that lobster will not curl up during grilling.

Drain oil from smoked oysters and empty them into a small bowl. Mash oysters with a wooden spoon. Cream with butter, softened at room temperature, adding lemon juice, chopped chives, mustard powder, Tabasco and Worcestershire sauce. Cover exposed lobster meat lightly with this spread.

Grill over medium bed of hot coals, flesh side down, for 5 minutes. Turn and again spread liberal portions of deviled butter on lobster. Grill 6 or 7 minutes, or until lobster meat is opaque. Overcooking will make lobster meat tough.

Remove lobster from grill. Heat any remaining spread and serve with lobster and lemon wedges. Small forks, nutcrackers, nut picks, a lobster bib for each person and hot, damp finger towels will be helpful and appreciated.

This will serve 2 as a main course. Or give 4 people half a lobster each and finish the meal with grilled yellowtail flounder fillets (see page 145).

Note: If lobster is frozen, thaw completely before grilling. Spread deviled butter on exposed lobster meat and wrap each lobster half in heavy duty foil, closing securely with a double fold. Place on grill over medium bed of hot coals, shell side down, for 15 minutes.

FLAMING LOBSTER

Frozen lobster tails	Marinade:
16 *small, fresh mushrooms*	⅓ *cup olive oil*
2 *Tbsps. butter*	⅓ *cup lime juice*
8 *slices Canadian bacon*	2 *Tbsps. grated lime rind*
2 *oz. brandy, warmed*	3 *Tbsps. chopped chives*
	1 *garlic clove, pressed*
	⅛ *tsp. cayenne pepper*
	1 *tsp. salt*

Number of tails will depend on their size. Total weight should be 2½ to 3 pounds. Or equivalent amount of meat from fresh or frozen whole lobsters can be used.

Completely thaw frozen lobster tails. Slit soft undershell with kitchen shears or sharp knife, remove meat and cut into 1-inch chunks. Marinate for at least a ½ hour in combined marinade ingredients at room temperature. Drain, reserving marinade.

Wash mushrooms, peel if necessary. Use caps only. Sauté gently for 5 minutes in butter. Cut Canadian bacon into squares similar to lobster chunks.

Skewer lobster meat, alternating with mushroom cap or bacon slice. Brush with marinade. Place on oiled grill over medium coals. Turn and baste frequently until lobster meat is golden, 7 or 8 minutes in all. Do not overcook.

Remove skewers to flameproof platter. Pour warmed brandy over top and ignite. Serve at once.

OYSTER STEW
(SKILLET)

2 doz. oysters, freshly shucked, with oyster liquor	1 Tbsp. Worcestershire sauce
	2-3 drops Tabasco sauce
	½ tsp. celery salt
2 cups clam juice	2 oz. dry sherry
¼ lb. butter, softened	2 cups cream, warmed
4 Tbsps. chili sauce	½ tsp. sweet paprika

Carefully remove any shell particles from oysters. Pour oyster liquor into clam juice.

In a deep pan over hot bed of coals, bring to boiling point 4 tablespoons butter, chili sauce, Worcestershire sauce, Tabasco and celery salt. Pour in clam juice, oyster liquor and sherry. When hot, add oysters and cook, stirring constantly, until edges of oysters begin to curl.

Pour in warm cream, heat until very hot. Sprinkle with paprika.

Pour into bowls, top each with pat of butter, and serve with heated pilot crackers.

TANDOORI SHRIMP

2 lbs. medium-size shrimp

Marinade:
2½ Tbsps. Tandoori spice	2 Tbsps. peanut oil
2 Tbsps. lime juice	2 Tbsps. water
1 Tbsp. sesame oil	

Shell, devein, rinse and dry shrimp.
Combine marinade ingredients into thick paste and rub thoroughly into shrimp. Let stand for several hours or refrigerate overnight.
Skewer and grill over medium hot coals for 4 or 5 minutes, turning to brown evenly.

Note: Tandoori spice is a blend of 9 special spices used in North India and Pakistan. It can be used equally effectively with chicken, lamb or fish. Monorama's Tandoori Spice comes in 2 and 5-ounce jars. If it is not available in your area, drop a card to the distributors, New Nations, Inc., 201 W. 98th St., New York, N.Y. 10025, asking where to get it.

SCAMPI
(IF YOU LIKE GARLIC! ! !)
(SKILLET)

2 lbs. jumbo shrimp (scampi or prawns)	pepper
½ cup olive oil	4 cloves of garlic, peeled
1 tsp. salt	½ cup finely chopped parsley

Peel, devein, wash, split and dry shrimp thoroughly.
In large, heavy skillet over high hot bed of glowing coals,

heat olive oil. Cook shrimp quickly, stirring and turning constantly, to sauté both sides. This should take no more than 6 or 7 minutes. Sprinkle with salt and a few good turns of the pepper mill and remove with slotted spoon to a heated platter.

With garlic press, squeeze 4 peeled cloves of garlic into hot oil, and cook, stirring, for 1 minute. Add minced parsley and stir another minute. Pour this sauce over shrimp and serve with hot French or Italian bread to sop up the juice.

BASQUE SHRIMP
(SKILLET)

2 lbs. medium-size shrimp
¼ cup sliced green olives
2 pimientos, sliced thin
½ tsp. salt
½ tsp. black pepper
3 Tbsps. olive oil

Sauce:
3 Tbsps. olive oil
2 Tbsps. butter
1 cup sweet onion, chopped fine
1 clove garlic, pressed
1 cup mushrooms, sliced thin
2 Tbsps. chopped parsley
1 medium-size can Italian plum tomatoes
½ tsp. crushed red peppers
½ tsp. salt
¼ tsp. dried basil
½ Tbsp. chili powder
1 tsp. sugar

SAUCE (can be made day before): Heat 3 tablespoons of olive oil and 2 tablespoons butter in heavy skillet over a low flame. Sauté onion, garlic, mushrooms and parsley for 10 minutes over a low flame. Add tomatoes and seasonings for sauce and simmer slowly for ½ hour. Correct seasonings, cool and store until ready to use.

Peel, devein, wash, split and thoroughly dry shrimp. Season with salt and pepper.

168 · FISH AND SEAFOOD

For tray: sauce, shrimp, olives, pimientos, salt, pepper mill and olive oil.

In large heavy skillet over high hot bed of glowing coals, heat 3 tablespoons of olive oil. Add shrimp and stir for 1 minute. Just as they begin to change color, pour in tomato sauce, adding sliced olives and pimiento strips. Cook until hot, stirring to prevent sticking or burning, at which time shrimp will be cooked through but still juicy. Serve bubbling hot.

GRILLED CURRIED SHRIMP WITH COCONUT CRUST

2 lbs. medium shrimp
1 cup moist shredded coconut

Marinade:
¼ cup olive oil
¼ cup of lime or lemon juice
1 Tbsp. Indian curry powder
1 tsp. chopped fresh mint
  or ¼ tsp. dry mint leaves
¼ tsp. crushed red peppers
1 small onion, grated

Shell, devein, wash and dry shrimp with paper towels.

Combine marinade ingredients and pour over shrimp in non-metal container. Marinate in refrigerator overnight.

Drain shrimp and thread on skewers. Reserve marinade.

Grill over hot coals for 4 minutes, turning to brown evenly. After 4 minutes, remove skewers from hibachi. Brush shrimp with marinade and roll each skewer in plate of shredded coconut. Return to coals and grill another minute, turning, just long enough to toast coconut.

CHARCOAL GRILLED SHRIMP À LA TAHITI

2 lbs. raw shrimp
1 cup unsweetened pineapple juice
⅓ cup soy sauce

3 Tbsps. honey
1 Tbsp. butter
½ tsp. powdered ginger
1½ Tbsps. cornstarch

Mix ¾ cup pineapple juice, soy sauce, honey, butter and ginger in saucepan. Bring to a boil and stir in cornstarch dissolved in ¼ cup pineapple juice. Let cool slightly.

Shell and devein shrimp. Pour sauce over them and mix until they are well coated. Allow shrimp to marinate in this sauce in refrigerator for several hours.

Arrange shrimp on skewers and broil over medium coals, 8 to 10 minutes, turning to brown evenly. Do not overcook.

SAFFRON SHRIMP
WITH COCONUT, BANANAS AND NUTS
(SKILLET)

2 lbs. medium-size shrimp
2 bananas, firm
3 Tbsps. lemon juice
3 Tbsps. butter
3 Tbsps. peanut oil
½ tsp. powdered saffron
1 Tbsp. cornstarch

2-3 drops Tabasco sauce
1 cup rich chicken broth
½ cup cream
¼ cup grated coconut
¼ cup slivered toasted almonds
salt and pepper

Shell, devein and split raw shrimp in half. Rinse and pat dry with paper towels.

Peel and slice bananas into ½-inch pieces and sprinkle with lemon juice. Cover bowl with plastic or wax paper to prevent discoloration.

In large, heavy skillet on hibachi grill, over high hot bed of glowing coals, heat butter and peanut oil. Add shrimp, stirring constantly, and cook for 3 or 4 minutes, or until they turn pink. Remove with slotted spoon to heated platter.

Drain lemon juice from bananas and add banana slices to skillet. Cook, turning to brown, for 2 minutes. Remove to platter with shrimp.

Stir saffron into skillet, scraping to loosen browned bits. Add cornstarch and Tabasco to chicken broth and pour into pan. Simmer until slightly thickened, add cream, then coconut and almonds. Season lightly with salt and pepper. Return shrimp and banana slices, heat through and serve at once.

SKEWERED SHRIMP AND CUCUMBERS WITH CURRIED PISTACHIO BUTTER

2 lbs. shrimp (good-size ones)
3 firm cucumbers

Marinade:	Basting and Serving Sauce:
1 cup white wine vinegar	*¼ lb. butter, melted*
or cider vingar	*1 Tbsp. lemon juice*
½ cup cold water	*1 ½ tsps. Indian curry*
1 tsp. salt	*powder*
1 clove garlic, minced	*¼ cup finely ground*
½ bay leaf, crumbled	*pistachio nuts*

Shell, devein, wash and dry shrimp. Marinate in non-metal container in refrigerator for 3 or 4 hours in combined vinegar, water, salt, garlic and bay leaf.

Deeply score unpeeled cucumbers by drawing a fork firmly from one end of cucumber to the other. Repeat all around each cucumber. Slice into ½-inch discs. Cover with boiling water for 5 minutes. Drain and dry thoroughly between paper towels. Store in the refrigerator in a plastic bag or covered bowl until ready to use.

Remove shrimp from marinade and skewer alternately with cucumber rounds, leaving small spaces between. Brush generously with butter melted and combined with lemon juice, curry powder and ground pistachios.

Grill over hot coals for 5 or 6 minutes, turning to brown evenly. Baste often with butter.

Remove from grill and serve with remaining warm butter sauce poured over top.

SHRIMP AND MUSSELS MEDITERRANEAN
(SKILLET)

1 ½ cups steamed and shelled mussels	½ tsp. basil
2 lbs. large shrimp	1 Tbsp. capers
½ cup cornmeal	1 cup tomato juice
2 Tbsps. butter	¼ cup tomato purée
4 Tbsps. olive oil	1 Tbsp. tomato paste
1 clove garlic, pressed	salt and pepper
1 tsp. oregano	1 Tbsp. chopped chives

To prepare mussels, scrub under cold running water with a stiff brush. Let stand in cold water to cover, to which you have added ½ cup of cornmeal. Wash thoroughly and steam mussels in small amount of water, discarding any which do not open readily. Remove mussels from shells and trim off any remaining beards.

Shell, devein and split raw shrimp in half. Rinse and dry thoroughly with paper towels.

In large, heavy skillet over high hot bed of glowing coals, heat butter and olive oil. Stir in pressed garlic, oregano, basil and capers. Add shrimp and sauté, stirring constantly with wooden spoon, for about 3 minutes, or until shrimp have turned pink. Add tomato juice, purée and paste and steamed mussels. Season with a few good turns of the pepper mill and a little salt. Simmer until heated through. Sprinkle with chives and serve at once.

SHRIMP AND SCALLOPS WITH CASHEWS
(SKILLET)

1 *lb. medium-size shrimp*
½ *lb. bay scallops*
2 *Tbsps. butter*
2 *Tbsps. olive oil*
6 *shallots, sliced fine*
 or 4 scallions, chopped fine
2 *Tbsps. tomato paste*
pinch of cayenne pepper
½ *cup cashew nuts, coarsely*
 chopped
pepper
¼ *cup finely chopped*
 parsley

Marinade:
⅓ *cup lemon juice*
⅓ *cup olive oil*
1 *clove garlic, pressed*
½ *tsp. salt*
¼ *cup dry white wine*
1 *tsp. tarragon*

Shell, devein and split raw shrimp in half lengthwise. Rinse and dry thoroughly. If bay scallops are not available, cut larger sea scallops in quarters. Carefully pick off any shell particles, rinse and dry. Cover cleaned shrimp and scallops with combined marinade ingredients in a non-metal bowl or container and let stand for at least an hour. Drain, reserving marinade.

In large, heavy skillet on hibachi grill, over high hot bed of glowing coals, heat butter and olive oil. Stir in well-drained shrimp and scallops and cook, stirring and turning, for 3 minutes. Remove with slotted spoon to hot platter.

Add shallots to skillet, stirring for 1 minute. Add tomato paste, cayenne and ½ cup of the reserved marinade. As soon as this starts to simmer, return the shrimp and scallops to skillet, heat thoroughly and stir in cashew nuts. Sprinkle with freshly ground black pepper and chopped parsley. Serve bubbling hot over hot boiled white rice.

SWEET AND PUNGENT SCALLOPS
(SKILLET)

1½ lbs. scallops (preferably bay)
4 Tbsps. kumquat syrup
4 Tbsps. cider vinegar
1 tsp. brandy
1 Tbsp. soy sauce
1 Tbsp. hoisin sauce
or 1½ Tbsps. catsup
1 Tbsp. cornstarch
1 cup beef consommé

4 Tbsps. peanut oil
salt and pepper
1 tsp. fresh minced ginger,
or ¼ tsp. powdered ginger
1 small 8-oz. jar preserved kumquats, drained and diced fine
¼ cup finely chopped scallions, including some of green

Carefully remove any shell particles from scallops. Rinse in cold water, drain and dry thoroughly with paper toweling. If bay scallops are unavailable, cut sea scallops in quarters.

Combine kumquat syrup, vinegar, brandy, soy sauce, hoisin or catsup. Dissolve cornstarch in a little of the cold beef consommé, then mix it thoroughly with rest of consommé and add to syrup-vinegar mixture. This can be brought to table on tray with scallops, diced kumquats, ginger, peanut oil, scallions, salt and pepper.

In large, heavy skillet on hibachi grill, over high hot bed of glowing coals, heat 3 tablespoons peanut oil. Sprinkle scallops sparingly with salt and pepper, and when oil is hot, stir in scallops, cooking and turning for a maximum of 2 or 3 minutes. Scallops toughen with overcooking. Remove scallops to heated platter.

Pour remaining tablespoon of peanut oil into skillet and when it is hot, add minced ginger root and diced kumquats. Cook, stirring, for 1 minute. Since cornstarch tends to settle, be sure to stir up sweet-sour sauce thoroughly, then add to kumquats in skillet. Simmer for 5 minutes, stirring, until slightly thickened. Return scallops to sauce and heat through (about 1 minute).

Serve at once sprinkled with chopped scallions.

MIXED SEAFOOD WITH MUSHROOMS AND GRUYÈRE
(SKILLET)

1 *lb. medium-size shrimp*
2 *medium-size lobster tails*
   (total about 1½ lbs.)
½ *lb. scallops (preferably*
   bay)
½ *lb. lump crab meat*
1 *cup finely chopped sweet*
   onions
1 *green pepper, cut into thin*
   strips

½ *lb. fresh mushrooms,*
   sliced thin
2 *Tbsps. chopped parsley*
8 *Tbsps. sweet butter*
2 *three-oz. packages cream*
   cheese
3 *half-oz. packages Swiss*
   Gruyère cheese
1 *cup tomato juice*
salt and pepper
4 *Tbsps. light olive oil*

Note: Sauce can be prepared in advance and kept warm in a double boiler. Or prepare it a day ahead without the cheese, then add cheese when the sauce is reheated.

SAUCE: Sauté onions, green pepper, mushrooms and parsley in 4 tablespoons butter until soft. Add cream cheese and Gruyère, cubed, and allow to melt over a very low flame. Thin sauce with 1 cup of tomato juice. Season to taste.

Shell, devein and split raw shrimp. Rinse and pat dry. If frozen, thaw lobster tails, split soft underside and cut into 1-inch pieces. Rinse scallops quickly, removing any bits of shell, and dry. If sea scallops are used, cut them into smaller pieces. Carefully pick over crab meat for shell or cartilage.

In large heavy skillet on hibachi grill, over high hot bed of glowing coals, heat 4 tablepoons butter and 4 tablespoons olive oil. When hot, add shrimp and lobster pieces. Sauté, stirring constantly with wooden spoon, for 3 or 4 minutes. Add scallops and cook an additional 2 minutes, stirring. Stir in crab meat and pour in warm sauce. If necessary, thin mixture with a few ounces of tomato juice. Heat until bubbling hot and serve at once with plain boiled white rice or noodles.

Serves 6 to 8.

DESSERTS

Desserts

Be sure hibachi grill is thoroughly clean before you make desserts on it.

.

GLAZED APPLE SLICES WITH CHEDDAR DIP

6 *small apples, firm and*
  juicy
4 *Tbsps. lemon juice*
¼ *cup honey*

Cheddar Dip:
8 oz. *sharp Cheddar cheese,*
  cubed
4 *Tbsps. heavy cream*
1 *tsp. prepared sharp*
  mustard
1 *tsp. grated horseradish*
1 *Tbsp. caraway seeds*

DIP: Soften cheese at room temperature and blend into smooth mixture with cream, mustard, horseradish and caraway seeds. If stored in refrigerator, remove several hours before using to soften and mellow.

Quarter and core unpeeled apples. Dip in lemon juice and brush with honey. Place on oiled hand-grill over medium low coals for about 5 minutes, turning to glaze. Apples should be crisp inside, so don't overcook.

Place bowl of Cheddar dip in center of serving plate. Place apple quarters around edges of plate, speared with sturdy cocktail picks.

Serve at once.

GRILLED APRICOTS

1 *large can of whole apricots*
4 *Tbsps. brown sugar*
2 *Tbsps. sherry*
4 *Tbsps. melted butter*

½ *cup graham cracker*
  crumbs, very fine
¼ *tsp. ground cloves*
¼ *tsp. ground cinnamon*

Drain and cut apricots in half, removing pit.

Make a paste of brown sugar and sherry. Spread on cut side of apricot halves, then press 2 halves together to make a whole apricot again. Brush generously with butter and roll in graham cracker crumbs mixed with cloves and cinnamon.

Skewer 4 apricots on each long thin skewer, spearing through to secure halves.

Remove grid from hibachi. Rest ends of skewers on sides of hibachi and broil apricots over low coals, turning to toast evenly. Grill for 5 or 6 minutes.

These are delicious plain or served with a bowl of cold whipped sweet cream or sour cream.

BANANA-PAPAYA FLAMBÉ
(SKILLET)

3 ripe firm bananas
2 Tbsps. lemon juice
½ tsp. cinnamon
6 Tbsps. butter, softened
3 Tbsps. brown sugar

4 tenderized apricots,
 chopped fine
2 Tbsps. grated lemon rind
1 small can sliced papaya,
 drained
¼ cup light rum, warmed

Peel and split bananas in half lengthwise; then cut into 1-inch pieces. Sprinkle with lemon juice and cinnamon.

In heavy skillet on grill over hot coals, melt butter and brown sugar. Stir in chopped apricots and lemon rind. Add banana and papaya slices. Sauté, turning carefully until well heated, but do not allow bananas to get too soft.

Pour warmed rum over fruit, ignite and serve at once.

BANANAS GRILLED IN THEIR SKINS

6 firm bananas
½ cup honey
4 Tbsps. sweet butter

juice of 2 limes
3 Tbsps. brown sugar
½ cup cognac, warmed

Blend honey with softened sweet butter. Make small slit in skin of each banana and force in 1/6 part of mixture.

Grill over hot charcoal 4 minutes on each side.

Remove from grill to heat-proof platter. Split skin completely to expose entire length of fruit. Sprinkle with lime

juice and brown sugar and pour ½ cup of warmed cognac over all. Ignite and serve immediately.
Serves 6.

CHERRIES JUBILEE
(SKILLET)

1 #2 *can pitted black Bing* *cherries*
1 *Tbsp. arrowroot or* *cornstarch*
1 *Tbsp. honey*

2 *Tbsps. finely chopped* *preserved ginger*
¼ *cup cherry brandy,* *warmed*
vanilla ice cream

Drain cherries, reserving syrup. Make a smooth paste of the arrowroot and several tablespoons of the syrup, gradually adding balance of syrup. Stir in honey.

Place heavy-bottomed pan or skillet on hibachi grill over medium hot bed of coals. Add syrup mixture, stirring constantly for 3 or 4 minutes. Add drained cherries and chopped ginger. Simmer, stirring, until heated through.

Pour on warmed cherry brandy, ignite and serve over vanilla ice cream.

Note: Kirsch or cognac may be substituted for cherry brandy.

SPICED NECTARINES AND NUTS WITH SOUR CREAM

8 *nectarines, firm and ripe*
1 *cup sauterne*
4 *Tbsps. butter*
4 *Tbsps. brown sugar*

½ *tsp. powdered cloves*
¼ *cup finely chopped nuts* *(almonds, hazelnuts)*
½ *pt. chilled sour cream*

Halve and pit nectarines. Poach gently for 10 minutes in sauterne. Cool, drain and peel, reserving liquid.

Let butter soften at room temperature and cream it with brown sugar and cloves. Put a heaping teaspoon of mixture in the hollow of each piece of fruit.

Place 4 filled halves on a lightly buttered strip (about 9 x 18) of heavy duty foil. Sprinkle with some of the reserved wine. Seal foil with a double fold and secure both ends. Repeat with rest of nectarine halves.

Put foil packages on grill over medium low coals for 15 minutes. Open packages, sprinkle with nuts.

Serve with a bowl of chilled sour cream.

GRILLED PEACHES WITH RASPBERRY SAUCE

4 *large ripe peaches*
   or 8 *preserved peach halves*
1 *Tbsp. lemon juice*

1 *box frozen raspberries*
4 *Tbsps. melted butter*

Cut fresh peaches in half, remove pits, and simmer for 10 minutes in a small amount of water in covered pan. Cool, drain and peel. Sprinkle with lemon juice.

Thaw frozen raspberries and mash berries slightly with fork. Keep cold until ready to serve.

Brush peach halves generously with melted butter and grill over medium coals until lightly browned and heated through. Turn carefully, brushing on more butter.

Remove to serving dish, ladle on raspberries and serve.

PEACHES IN FOIL

1 *large can of sliced Elberta*
   peaches
juice of 1 *lemon*
¼ *cup cognac*

½ *tsp. ground nutmeg*
4 *Tbsps. brown sugar*
sour cream

Drain juice from large can of sliced peaches. Spread slices on double layer of double duty foil.

Sprinkle with lemon juice, cognac, nutmeg and brown sugar.

Seal carefully in foil. Package can be set on top of grill over low coals while you're eating dinner, for anywhere from 25 minutes to an hour.

Open up foil and ladle fruit into individual dishes. Top with cold sour cream.

PEARS WITH A TOUCH OF ORANGE

8 *large preserved pear halves with syrup*
juice of 2 large thin-skinned oranges
juice of 1 lime
rind from oranges and lime

¼ *tsp. powdered ginger*
4 *Tbsps. brown sugar*
2 *Tbsps. melted butter*
4 *Tbsps. Triple Sec or other orange liqueur, warmed*

Drain pear halves and reserve syrup.

With a small, sharp knife, cut slivers of skin from oranges and lime (without white pulpy part). Cover rinds with boiling water and let stand for 5 minutes. Drain.

Combine juice from oranges and lime with ginger, brown sugar and ¼ cup of pear juice; pour over rind and simmer slowly for about 10 minutes. Watch carefully, stirring occasionally, to prevent sticking or burning. When mixture is thick and syrupy, remove from heat.

Spoon some of syrup mixture on cut side of pear halves, press halves together and baste outside with syrup. Lay 2 joined pear halves on buttered piece of heavy duty foil and seal securely with double fold.

Place foiled packages on grill over medium bed of coals for 12 to 15 minutes, turning once.

Transfer pears carefully from packages to serving dish, pouring over any syrup in packet. Pour on warmed orange liqueur, ignite and serve at once.

GRILLED FRESH PINEAPPLE WITH MINT

1 medium-size ripe pineapple   ½ cup shredded coconut,
½ cup honey   toasted
4 Tbsps. finely chopped fresh
   mint

Quarter pineapple lengthwise. Remove hard center core. With a grapefruit knife, cut the meat of the pineapple from the shell in one piece. Slash each of these quarters into ½-inch slices across, but don't cut all the way through.

Combine honey with chopped mint and brush on each pineapple quarter, letting a little of the honey slide down between the slices.

Wrap each quarter securely in a lightly oiled double thickness of heavy foil. Place packages directly on bed of medium hot coals for 18 or 20 minutes, turning once.

Open packages on individual serving plates, sprinkle with toasted coconut and serve at once.

GOLDEN RUM PINEAPPLE
(SKILLET)

1 large ripe pineapple   ½ cup light rum
½ cup sweet butter   1 cup heavy cream
4 Tbsps. brown sugar

Prepare pineapple by peeling, coring and cutting into ½-inch cubes.

In heavy skillet or pan on hibachi grill, over medium hot coals, heat butter. Sauté diced pineapple until lightly browned. Sprinkle brown sugar and rum over fruit. Simmer for 2 minutes, stirring. Add heavy cream, heat through and serve.

Serves 6.

ROASTED CHESTNUTS

1 *lb. fresh chestnuts*   1 *Tbsp. salad oil*

With a small sharp-pointed knife, cut 2 gashes in the form of an X on the flat side of each chestnut.

Spread chestnuts out on a lightly oiled cookie sheet or flat pan and heat in a 350° oven for 15 minutes. This can be done well ahead of time.

Over low bed of burned-down coals spread chestnuts on grill. Roast for 20 to 25 minutes, turning once or twice.

These make a wonderful after-dinner snack.

ALTERNATE METHOD FOR ROASTING CHESTNUTS

Prepare chestnuts in oven as above.

Wrap, 8 to 10 chestnuts to a package, tight in lightly oiled pieces of foil. Place packages directly on coals. Grill for about 15 minutes, turning once or twice.

NUTS ROASTED IN THEIR SHELLS

Use walnuts, Brazil nuts, filberts or any combination of your favorite nuts in their shells.

Crack shells well but do not remove. Foil-wrap packages, including several nuts of each variety. Fold and seal tightly and lay on a bed of low coals. Roast for 10 minutes, turning packages once.

Lift from coals with tongs.

Serve as an extra dessert treat with fruit and cheese.

CRÈME DE CACAO SAUCE WITH COFFEE ICE CREAM
(SKILLET)

coffee ice cream
2 Tbsps. butter
3 oz. bitter chocolate
2 Tbsps. strong black coffee
4 Tbsps. confectioner's sugar

1 tsp. vanilla
4 Tbsps. heavy cream
4 oz. crème de Cacao,
  warmed

Melt butter in heavy-bottomed saucepan on hibachi grill over hot bed of coals. Add bitter chocolate, coffee, sugar and vanilla. Stir constantly until chocolate has melted. Add heavy cream, stirring until hot.

Add warmed liqueur, ignite, and stir until flames die.

Serve immediately, ladling generously over individual portions of coffee ice cream.

TOASTED POUND CAKE

Cut a homemade or good quality bakery pound cake into half-inch slices. Butter each slice on both sides, place in a hand-grill, and toast cake lightly on both sides.

Served with tea or coffee, this is a refreshing end to dinner.

HOT MINIATURE DANISH PASTRIES

You have used the hibachi for grilled hors d'oeuvres. Dinner is over and it is coffee-time. The coals have burned down to a low bed.

Place a sheet of foil over the grill, butter it lightly, and lay on it 3 or 4 assorted miniature Danish pastries for each guest.

When the pastries are good and hot, let each person select his favorite (with a pair of small tongs).

SPECIAL SUPPLEMENT

Special Supplement

The following special dishes are suggested accompaniments for hibachi-cooked food. They are not, themselves, necessarily made on the hibachi.

These recipes require no last-minute preparation. Many of them can be made ahead of time.

ICED GARDEN-YOGHURT SOUP

1 *bunch of scallions*
1 *bunch of red radishes*
1 *green pepper*
3 *small cucumbers*
4 *ripe tomatoes*
1 *clove garlic*
3 *Tbsps. olive oil*
¼ *cup chopped parsley*
3 *Tbsps. fresh dill*
　or 1½ *Tbsps. dried dill*
　weed

1 *Tbsp. fresh tarragon*
　or 1 *tsp. dried tarragon*
4 *half-pint containers of plain*
　yoghurt
½ *cup tomato juice*
½ *cup light sweet cream*
½ *cup sour cream*
1½ *tsp. salt*
freshly ground black pepper

Clean scallions and cut into 1-inch lengths, including green stems. Wash and stem radishes. Wash, quarter and remove seeds from green pepper. Peel cucumbers and cut into 1-inch pieces. Wash, stem and quarter tomatoes. Peel garlic.

Pour olive oil into bowl of blender and begin process of puréeing the vegetables and herbs. Don't put too many vegetables in at a time; blend at high speed until puréed, then scrape contents out of blender into a large bowl. Always start a new batch with yoghurt, cream or some tomato juice at the bottom. When all the vegetables and herbs have been blended, quickly blend whatever yoghurt, juice or cream has not been used and mix everything thoroughly in bowl. Season with salt and pepper. Add 6 or 8 ice cubes. Cover bowl tightly and refrigerate, overnight if possible.

Before serving, stir well and, if necessary, correct seasoning. If too thick for your taste, add a little more tomato juice or several ice cubes.

This is a first-rate hot weather soup. It's nice served in coffee mugs.

Will serve 8.

PIROZHKI

Pastry:
¼ *lb. butter*
¼ *lb. cream cheese*
1 *cup sifted flour*

Filling:
½ *lb. lean beef, ground twice*
1 *medium-size onion,*
  chopped
6 *fresh mushrooms, chopped*
  fine
2 *Tbsps. butter*
1 *tsp. salt*
½ *tsp. pepper*
1 *hard-boiled egg, chopped*
  fine
1 *tsp. paprika*
2 *Tbsps. sour cream*

PASTRY: Have butter and cream cheese at room temperature. Combine them with fork. Cut in sifted flour with pastry blender or 2 knives. Work with hands until dough holds together. Form into ball, wrap in waxed paper and chill, preferably overnight.

FILLING: Sauté chopped onion and mushrooms in butter. Season ground meat with salt and pepper and brown in same pan with onions and mushrooms. Add egg. Stir paprika into sour cream and add to mixture, correcting seasoning if necessary.

Roll out dough (a third of it at one time) on a generously floured board. Roll as thin as possible. Cut into circles about 2½ inches in diameter. Place 1 teaspoon of filling in center, fold over once, pinching edges together. Place each pirozhok as it is finished on a floured cookie sheet.

Preheat oven to 425° and bake pirozhki for 15 minutes or until crust is delicately browned.

Note: These can be prepared ahead of time and stored unbaked on covered cookie sheet in refrigerator until 15 minutes before ready to serve. Bake as above.

FLUFFY WHITE RICE

Rice is an excellent accompaniment for many dishes. To cook it properly is simple, yet it is amazing how many cooks manage to make it look and taste like boiled glue.

"Converted" long grain rice is already processed and needs no washing or rinsing. If the package directions are followed exactly (with the possible exception of omitting salt), this rice will approximate regular long grain rice prepared in the Oriental way.

Whichever rice you use, it should be served fluffy and dry, with each grain separate and cooked through.

There are many theories about cooking "plain rice," from using various finger joints or other measures for water level above rice to plunging raw rice into gallons of wildly seething water.

However, the safest way to turn out a respectable bowl of rice is by measuring accurately and using a heavy pot with a tight cover, deep enough to accommodate the increased bulk of the rice as it cooks. A little lemon juice added to the cooking water will make the rice even whiter.

Yield

1 cup of regular long grain rice — 3 cups cooked rice
1 cup of "converted" long grain rice — 4 cups cooked rice

Salt is omitted from rice when served with Oriental dishes.

If rice is being served with grilled foods that are without sauce or seasoning, for each cup of raw rice, substitute for water:
1 ¾ cups of chicken broth
      or beef consommé
      or onion soup (from package)
For "converted" rice, use water substitute in proper ratio.

Top of Stove Method

1 *cup long grain rice*
1 ¾ *cups cold water*
1 *tsp. lemon juice*

Rice must be thoroughly washed before cooking to remove excess starch. Otherwise, it will burn quickly and have a gummy texture. Place rice in a strainer over a pot and wash under cold running water until water runs clear. Then to be sure, wash it again. Drain. Place in pot with the exact amount of cold water and lemon juice, and bring to a boil, uncovered. Immediately cover pan tightly, turn flame very low and FORGET it for 20 minutes. Don't peek and don't stir. At the end of 20 minutes, turn off the flame, and let rice stand, covered, for another 20 minutes. Stir lightly with fork to separate grains and serve.

Oven Method

1 *cup long grain rice*
1 ¾ *cups cold water*
1 *tsp. lemon juice*

Wash and drain rice, as for top of stove method. Preheat oven to 350°. Place rice, water and lemon juice in covered casserole and bake for 40 minutes. Check, stir with fork. If too dry, add a few tablespoons of water. Turn oven to 325° and bake, uncovered, for 5 to 10 minutes.

ORANGE RICE WITH MINT

1½ cups white rice
½ cup finely chopped onion
4 Tbsps. butter
4 Tbsps. grated orange rind
salt and pepper

3 cups chicken broth
¾ cup orange juice
1 Tbsp. fresh mint, chopped
  or ½ tsp. dry mint leaves
½ cup pignolia nuts

Sauté chopped onion in butter until soft. Stir in raw rice. Add grated orange rind, a little salt and some freshly ground pepper. Combine with chicken broth, orange juice and mint in an ovenproof casserole.

In a preheated 325° oven, cook rice, uncovered, for 1 hour. Add a little chicken broth or water if rice becomes too dry. In last 10 minutes, mix in pignolia nuts.

If, at the end of an hour, rice is not done, turn oven up to 375°, cover casserole loosely with foil, and cook an additional 5 to 10 minutes.

If you have to keep rice hot after it has finished cooking, turn oven to lowest heat and cover casserole to keep rice from drying out.

SAVORY BROWN RICE WITH GIBLETS

1 cup natural brown rice
½ cup chicken giblets
½ cup finely chopped onions
¼ cup finely chopped green
  pepper

2 Tbsps. butter
1 tsp. salt
½ tsp. black pepper
½ tsp. thyme
3 cups chicken broth

Simmer chicken giblets until tender in slightly salted water to cover. Drain and chop.

Sauté chopped onions and green pepper in 2 tablespoons butter until soft. Season with salt, pepper and thyme. Add raw rice and stir long enough to coat.

Transfer rice to ovenproof casserole. Stir in chicken broth

and chopped giblets. Cover casserole and bake in 350° pre-heated oven for 1 hour. Stir once or twice during this period, adding a little additional broth or hot water if rice becomes too dry. If rice is not thoroughly cooked at the end of an hour, remove lid and bake an additional 5 to 10 minutes.

Note: If rice must be held after it is ready, turn heat to lowest level and keep casserole covered.

VERY SPECIAL RICE
(also foolproof)

¼ cup dried currants	white wine
2 cups long grain rice	¼ cup slivered almonds
2 oz. sweet butter	¼ cup pignolia nuts
2 oz. olive oil	3 small pimientos, sliced thin
2 medium onions, minced fine	1 Tbsp. salt
6 shallots, minced	1 tsp. freshly ground pepper
¼ cup chopped parsley	1 tsp. powdered saffron
1 green pepper, chopped	¼ tsp. grated nutmeg
½ lb. mushrooms, peeled and sliced	5 cups strong chicken broth

Soften the currants in enough white wine to cover; drain.

In a large iron skillet over medium heat, melt the butter. Add the olive oil and heat.

Add the onions, shallots, parsley, green pepper and sauté slowly. When vegetables are soft, add the mushrooms.

Add currants with almonds, pignolia nuts and pimientos. Stir in the salt, pepper, saffron and nutmeg.

Add the rice and stir until the grains are thoroughly coated. Spread the mixture in a shallow earthenware dish or casserole. Pour in the chicken broth and stir through.

Cook uncovered in a 350° oven for 50 to 60 minutes. Add a small amount of chicken broth or water, if necessary.

Serves 8.

SAVORY WILD RICE

1 cup wild rice	3 Tbsps. butter
3 Tbsps. minced shallots	½ tsp. salt
1 celery stalk, chopped fine	¼ tsp. black pepper
½ cup thinly sliced	¼ tsp. powdered marjoram
mushrooms	2 cups strong chicken broth

Wash rice well in at least 3 or 4 changes of cold water, discarding any husks which float to the surface. Drain well. Boil vigorously for 5 minutes in 2 quarts of rapidly boiling water. Skim scum from top of water, drain rice and spread it out on a cookie sheet or absorbent paper to dry thoroughly.

Sauté shallots, celery and mushrooms in butter for 5 minutes. Season with salt, pepper and marjoram. Combine with dried rice in a heavy ovenproof casserole. Stir in chicken broth, cover tightly and bake for 45 minutes in a preheated 350° oven. If rice becomes too dry, add a little chicken broth or hot water.

When ready to serve, toss with 2 forks to separate grains.

PILAF OF GROATS AND MUSHROOMS
(Kasha)

1 cup brown buckwheat	6 Tbsps. butter
groats	1 tsp. freshly ground pepper
1 egg	2½ cups strong chicken
1 tsp. salt	broth
1 medium onion, chopped	1 cup sliced mushrooms
fine	

Beat egg until foamy and stir with salt into groats.

Sauté chopped onion in 1 tablespoon butter until soft. Add pepper and 3 tablespoons butter. When butter is hot, stir in groats. Cook over moderate heat, stirring, for 10 minutes.

Preheat oven to 400°. Transfer groats and onion mixture to ovenproof casserole, stir in 2 cups of the chicken broth, cover tightly and bake in oven for 30 minutes.

Meanwhile, sauté sliced mushrooms in 2 tablespoons butter until soft. When groats have cooked at 400° for 30 minutes, turn heat down to 300°. Stir sautéed mushrooms and remaining chicken broth into groats, cover casserole, and return to oven for an additional 25 to 30 minutes. Check occasionally. If mixture becomes too dry, stir in a little hot water.

Groats should be tender and moist, but not mushy.

HUNGARIAN-STYLE NOODLES
WITH SPINACH AND CHEESE

1 8-oz. pkg. medium egg
    noodles
1 onion, minced fine
4 Tbsps. butter
1 tsp. salt
½ tsp. white pepper
1 Tbsp. paprika

1 Tbsp. flour
1½ cups cream
3 cups cooked, drained and
    chopped spinach (fresh
    or frozen)
1 cup Parmesan or Romano
    cheese, coarsely grated

Cook noodles, rinse with cold water and drain well.

Sauté onion in 2 tablespoons of butter. When soft but not brown, season with salt, pepper and paprika, and add 2 remaining tablespoons of butter. Make a thin paste with the flour and some of the cream, mix with remaining cream, and stir into seasoned onions. Simmer, stirring, until thickened, then blend in spinach. Correct seasoning if necessary.

In a well-buttered ovenproof dish, spread a layer of cooked drained noodles, sprinkle with grated cheese, cover with a layer of spinach mixture. Repeat layers, ending with a layer of noodles and a generous sprinkling of cheese on top.

Bake in a preheated 375° oven for approximately 15 minutes, or until cheese is browned and everything is very hot.

Note: This can be made well in advance and reheated. In this case, put casserole into a cold oven, turn heat to 350° for 15 minutes, then increase to 375° for an additional 10 minutes.

HIBACHI NOODLES ALFREDO
(SKILLET)

1 lb. narrow egg noodles
¼ lb. sweet butter, melted
⅓ cup grated Parmesan
   cheese

¼ cup grated Romano cheese
¼ cup heavy cream, warmed
pepper

Cook noodles according to package directions. Rinse, drain well and keep warm in colander over hot water.

In large deep pan on grill over medium bed of glowing coals, pour in enough of the butter to cover bottom of pan. Transfer noodles from colander to pan and pour on remaining butter. Toss the noodles constantly, to coat thoroughly with the butter, and start adding the cheese. After all the cheese has been added, continue tossing, pouring in the warmed cream, a little at a time.

When all the noodles are well coated and very hot, finish with a few generous twists of the pepper mill and serve at once.

FARMER CHEESE NUGGETS

1 lb. dry farmer cheese
3 eggs, beaten
3 Tbsps. melted butter
3 Tbsps. fine cracker meal
½ tsp. salt

1 cup dry fine bread crumbs
1 tsp. onion salt
1 Tbsp. finely chopped
   parsley

Force farmer cheese through a sieve. Combine it with beaten eggs, melted butter and cracker meal. Add salt. Let mixture stand, covered, in refrigerator for 3 to 4 hours.

Form mixture into small walnut-size nuggets and drop into rapidly boiling water. Poach for 6 or 7 minutes, 6 or 8 nuggets at a time. Remove with a slotted spoon.

Roll cheese balls in bread crumbs seasoned with onion salt and chopped parsley, and bake in 1 layer in large buttered pan for 15 to 20 minutes in a 350° oven. Turn once to brown evenly.

Note: Everything can be prepared ahead of time, ready to go into preheated oven 20 minutes before serving time.

LIMA BEAN AND APPLE CASSEROLE

2 cups dried baby lima beans
¼ lb. salt pork
1 small onion
3 cloves
1 clove garlic
herb bouquet (in cheesecloth bag)
  4 sprigs parsley
  1 bay leaf
  ½ tsp. thyme
1 cup chopped onions

1 cup peeled and sliced tart green apples
4 Tbsps. butter
½ cup white wine
1½ cups bean stock
1 tsp. salt
1 tsp. allspice
½ tsp. black pepper
4 lean strips of bacon
¼ cup finely chopped parsley

Bring 2 quarts of water to the boiling point, drop dried lima beans in pot, and after water has returned to boil, cook for 2 minutes. Remove from heat and soak beans in this pot overnight.

Simmer salt pork in boiling water to cover for 10 minutes. Drain and dice fine.

To COOK BEANS: Add enough cold water to pot in which beans have soaked to bring level of water 1 inch over top of beans. Add diced salt pork, onion with cloves stuck in it, garlic and herb bouquet. Cover and simmer slowly for at least 1 hour or until limas are almost done. Discard garlic, herb bouquet and onion. Drain, reserving bean stock.

Sauté chopped onions and apple slices in butter until soft. Add to drained beans with wine and 2 cups of bean stock in an ovenproof casserole. Taste and add salt if necessary. Stir in allspice and black pepper. Criss-cross bacon strips on top.

Bake in a preheated 350° oven for 1 hour, adding more bean stock if it becomes too dry. If beans are not tender, cook another 5 or 10 minutes. Add chopped parsley at serving time.

BAKED CHICK-PEAS
(Garbanzos)

2 cups dried chick-peas	½ Tbsp. chili powder
½ Tbsp. salt	¼ lb. peperoni sausage,
½ bay leaf	skinned and sliced
2 Tbsps. olive oil	2 Tbsps. cider vinegar
1 clove garlic, pressed	1 cup stewed tomatoes
1 cup onions, chopped	

Soak chick-peas overnight in cold water 2 to 3 inches above level of peas.

To cook, place chick-peas and water in heavy saucepan with salt, crumbled bay leaf and add enough cold water to the water in the pot to keep a level 2 to 3 inches above peas. Bring to boil, cover, and simmer slowly until almost tender, about 2 hours.

Heat olive oil in heavy skillet, add pressed garlic, chopped onions and chili powder. Stir to mix and sauté 5 minutes. Add sliced sausage and cook gently for 15 minutes. Stir in vinegar and tomatoes.

Drain chick-peas, reserving stock. Pour drained chick-peas into casserole, add onion-tomato mixture and 1½ cups of bean stock. Stir to blend all ingredients, and bake, covered, in preheated 325° oven for an hour. Check once or twice and add more stock if mixture becomes too dry.

SPECIAL EGGPLANT CASSEROLE

3 *small eggplants*
1 *large Bermuda onion*
2 *stalks celery*
1 *green pepper*
1/4 *lb. fresh mushrooms*
1 *small cucumber*
4 *very small zucchini squash*
4 *medium-size fresh ripe*
  tomatoes

2 *small carrots*
1/4 *cup olive oil*
1 *clove garlic*
salt and pepper to taste
1 *Tbsp. oregano*
3 *Tbsps. lemon juice*
1/4 *cup finely chopped*
  parsley
1/4 *cup grated Parmesan*
  cheese

Vegetable preparation:

Eggplant: Peel and cut into 1/2-inch cubes.

Onion and celery: Chop fine.

Green Pepper: Wash, remove seeds and cut into 1/4-inch strips, lengthwise.

Mushrooms: Wash, peel if necessary, and cut into thin slices.

Cucumber: Peel, quarter lengthwise, remove seeds and cut diagonally into 1/2-inch slices.

Zucchini: Trim ends, scrub well, and cut into 1/4-inch round slices.

Tomatoes: Peel and quarter.

Carrots: Scrape and slice into ribbon strips with potato peeler.

Heat half the olive oil in heavy casserole over medium flame. Press in garlic clove, stir for a few seconds, then quickly sauté cubed eggplant. When lightly browned, remove with slotted spoon. Add more olive oil. When hot, sauté onion, celery, green pepper and mushrooms. Cook for 4 or 5 minutes, stirring several times. Add cucumber, zucchini, tomatoes and carrots. Sauté a few minutes. Return browned eggplant cubes to casserole. Season with salt, pepper and oregano. Pour in lemon juice. Stir to mix thoroughly.

Cover casserole tightly and bake in a 325° oven for 1 1/2 hours. Check seasoning; correct if necessary. Stir in chopped parsley, sprinkle top with grated cheese and return to oven, uncovered, for an additional 15 minutes.

NOTE: Dish is now ready to serve but can be kept warm by turning oven down as low as possible.

If any of this casserole is left, it will keep under refrigeration for several days. Serve it chilled, sprinkled with a little lemon juice and olive oil.

BAKED PEPPERS WITH TOMATOES AND ANCHOVIES

3 medium-size sweet green peppers
3 medium-size sweet red peppers
12 small cherry tomatoes
4 Tbsps. olive oil
3 Tbsps. sweet butter, softened

2 Tbsps. finely chopped chives
1 Tbsp. finely chopped parsley
1 small clove garlic, pressed
24 rolled anchovy fillets, with capers
pepper
lemon wedges

Wash, cut peppers into quarters lengthwise. Wash and halve tomatoes.

Cover bottom of a large flat baking dish with 2 tablespoons of olive oil. With skin side down, arrange alternate red and green pepper quarters in a single layer in oiled dish.

Blend softened butter with chopped chives, parsley and pressed garlic. Spoon a little of this mixture on each pepper quarter, and top with a half tomato. Place an anchovy roll on tomato. Season generously with freshly ground pepper and sprinkle with remaining olive oil.

Bake in preheated 325° oven for 45 minutes. Remove and cool. Serve at room temperature with lemon wedges.

BAKED CURRIED CHESTNUTS

1 ½ lbs. chestnuts
1 cup chopped onion
2 tart apples, peeled and
    chopped
3 Tbsps. butter
1 Tbsp. Indian curry powder
2 Tbsps. flour

1 Tbsp. dark brown sugar
3 Tbsps. chopped raisins
2 cups chicken stock or
    consommé
salt
½ tsp. black pepper

To PREPARE CHESTNUTS: With a small sharp-pointed knife, make 2 gashes, in the form of an X, on the flat side of each chestnut. Place on a lightly oiled cookie sheet in a preheated 350° oven for 15 minutes. It should be possible to remove both the outer shell and the inner skin. If not, bake for another 5 minutes. Drop shelled chestnuts into enough salted boiling water to cover chestnuts by at least 1 inch. Simmer for 15 minutes.

Sauté onion and apples in butter until soft. Sprinkle with combined curry and flour. Stir in brown sugar and chopped raisins and slowly add chicken stock, stirring to mix well. Simmer until mixture thickens slightly.

Drain chestnuts, season with salt and pepper, and combine with curry broth in a tightly covered casserole. Bake in a preheated 325° oven for 1 hour. If mixture becomes too dry, add a little chicken stock or hot water.

ACCOMPANIMENTS FOR CURRY DISHES

Here are some relishes to serve with curries. It is traditional to have some, and you may use as many as you like. Each should be served in a separate bowl with its own serving spoon. Bowls should be grouped near the main dish so that each person can serve himself. It is helpful to identify the various dishes as guests are making selections.

Chutney

Major Grey's is the best known and most readily available, but there are many varieties of sweet and hot chutneys in shops specializing in spices and curries.

Blender Chutney

Put the following ingredients into blender bowl, some of each at a time, blend for a few seconds, add more and repeat:

8 *pitted dates*   4 *preserved kumquats*
2 *ripe bananas, sliced*   3 *or* 4 *Tbsps. kumquat syrup*
¼ *cup shredded coconut*   1 *Tbsp. lime or lemon juice*
½ *tsp. crushed red peppers*

Red Onions

One red onion, sliced paper thin, covered with 3 tablespoons red wine vinegar in shallow dish.

Toasted Garlic Almonds

Sauté 1 cup slivered blanched almonds in 3 tablespoons butter into which you have pressed ½ clove garlic. Stir constantly for 3 minutes over medium heat until almonds have browned but not burned. Remove from heat and stir an additional minute or 2. Salt slightly.

Sherried Raisins

Chop 1 cup seedless raisins coarse. Mix ¼ teaspoon each of mace and powdered ginger with enough dry sherry to cover raisins. Let stand overnight to soften. Drain excess liquid.

Chopped Peppers

Dice, as fine as possible, 1 sweet green pepper and 1 sweet red pepper. Combine with 2 finely chopped scallions.

Avocado and Pimiento

Peel and dice 1 large avocado. Sprinkle with lime juice to prevent discoloring. Mix with 2 finely diced pimientos and 4 tablespoons finely chopped chives. Season with ½ teaspoon salt and freshly ground pepper. Add 1 tablespoon grated lime rind and cover with 2 tablespoons olive oil.

Hard-boiled Eggs and Bacon
Chop 2 egg whites fine and combine with 2 sieved egg yolks and 2 slices of bacon, fried crisp and crumbled fine. Season with ¼ teaspoon white pepper.

Toasted Shredded Coconut
Spread coconut, shredded, on flat pan. Brown in 350° preheated oven until golden, about 10 minutes, stirring frequently and taking care not to burn.

Chili Peanuts
Combine 1 cup finely chopped peanuts with 1 teaspoon chili powder. Spread on flat pan and brown in preheated 350° oven for 5 minutes.

Fresh Pineapple
Combine 1 cup fresh pineapple, cut into small dice, with 1 tablespoon freshly chopped mint.

Peaches and Nuts
Combine ½ cup finely chopped brandied peaches with ¼ cup toasted almonds. Add enough brandied peach syrup to give it a chutney-like texture. Stir in ¼ teaspoon powdered ginger.

RADISH RELISH

3 bunches red radishes
½ green pepper, chopped
    fine
1 small onion, grated
1 large ripe tomato, peeled
    and chopped fine
½ tsp. salt

¼ cup lime or lemon juice
¼ cup olive oil
½ tsp. sugar
1 Tbsp. finely chopped fresh
    mint
    or ½ tsp. dry mint leaves

Stem, wash and slice radishes paper thin. Mix with green pepper, onion and tomato. Sprinkle with salt and let stand for ½ hour. Drain, pressing out excess juice.

Combine lime juice, olive oil, sugar and mint. Pour over vegetables in covered pottery or glass bowl. Store and chill. This relish can be made the day before. The flavor improves if left to stand a day or two.

MARINATED ASPARAGUS SPEARS WITH BEEFSTEAK TOMATOES

24 *fat stalks of tender asparagus*
3 *ripe beefsteak tomatoes*
1 *canned whole pimiento*

¼ *cup very finely chopped fresh basil*
salt and pepper
⅓ *cup olive oil*
4 *Tbsps. wine vinegar*

Remove woody ends of asparagus and steam or cook in your favorite way—but *undercook* it slightly. Slice tomatoes in thick rounds.

On a large platter, separate asparagus into bundles of 6 spears. Cut pimiento into strips. Spread a strip of pimiento across middle of each bunch. Between the bunches lay tomato slices.

Pound basil with a little salt until it is thoroughly mashed. Add oil, vinegar, salt to taste and pepper. Pour over asparagus and tomato slices and allow to marinate for an hour or so at room temperature. This should not be served chilled.

NOTE: This platter has the advantage of serving both as a salad and a vegetable. Bunches of slightly undercooked whole string beans can also be served this way. If fresh basil is unavailable, substitute your favorite oil-vinegar dressing for above.

AVOCADO-TOMATO MOUSSE RING

2 medium-size ripe avocados
2 envelopes unflavored
    gelatine
¾ cup tomato juice
2 cans condensed tomato soup
2 three-oz. pkgs. cream
    cheese
½ cup grated onion
½ cup finely chopped green
    pepper
3 hard-boiled eggs, chopped
    fine
1 tsp. salt
¾ cup mayonnaise
¼ cup chili sauce
parsley or watercress

Sprinkle gelatine on top of tomato juice. Heat undiluted tomato soup, add gelatine-tomato juice and stir until dissolved. Cool.

Peel, seed and mash avocadoes. Blend well with softened cream cheese. Add to cooled soup mixture.

Stir in grated onions, chopped pepper, hard-boiled eggs and salt.

Add mayonnaise and chili sauce. Blend well and pour into a slightly oiled 1½-quart ring mold. Chill until set.

At serving time, unmold on a large plate and decorate with parsley or watercress.

THREE-BEAN SALAD

2 cans red kidney beans, 1 lb.
    size
1 can garbanzos (chick-
    peas), 1 lb. size
¾ lb. young green string
    beans
6 scallions, including greens,
    sliced thin
4 tender inner celery stalks,
    sliced thin

Dressing:
½ cup olive oil
¼ cup white wine vinegar
3 Tbsps. lemon juice
½ clove garlic, pressed
1 Tbsp. fresh basil, chopped
    or 1 tsp. dried basil
1 Tbsp. chopped fresh
    tarragon
    or 1 tsp. dried tarragon
salt and pepper

Drain kidney beans and garbanzos and rinse under running cold water. Cut string beans in 1-inch pieces. Slightly undercook them so they will be crisp. Cool. Mix kidney beans, garbanzos, string beans, scallions and celery in a pottery, glass or plastic bowl.

Combine dressing ingredients and pour over salad. Mix well. Cover bowl and chill thoroughly. Toss just before serving. This salad improves with longer marinating and should be made well ahead of time.

Note: Other types of beans such as black beans, baby limas, yellow wax beans or others can be added or substituted, but the texture contrast of at least one fresh crisp type of bean with the "dried" bean is important.

LENTIL SALAD

3 cups cooked lentils
½ cup finely chopped red
    onions
½ cup peeled and cubed tart
    apples
2 small pickled herring
    fillets, slivered
2 sweet pimientos, in thin
    strips

1 celery stalk, chopped fine
4 Tbsps. lime or lemon juice
6 Tbsps. olive oil
½ tsp. mustard powder
½ tsp. freshly ground pepper
1 Tbsp. chopped parsley
salt
watercress or lettuce

Cook lentils according to package directions. Drain thoroughly and cool. Combine with chopped onions, apples, herring, pimientos and celery.

Mix lime juice, olive oil, mustard, pepper and parsley and blend well with lentil mixture. Salt to taste. Chill. (This salad can be prepared the day before because its flavor improves as it marinates.) Serve on a bed of watercress or lettuce.

WATERCRESS AND SPINACH SALAD
WITH SESAME DRESSING

1 *bunch young watercress*
1 *lb. young small spinach*
3 *Tbsps. finely chopped*
   chives

Sesame Dressing:
¼ *cup sesame seeds*
   or 2 Tbsps. sesame oil
2 *Tbsps. mild vinegar*
2 *Tbsps. lemon juice*
1 *tsp. sugar*
1 *Tbsp. soy sauce*
½ *tsp. MSG or Accent*
¼ *cup peanut oil*

Remove stems from watercress and spinach. Wash thoroughly and dry completely. Chill.

SESAME DRESSING: In heavy ungreased iron skillet toast sesame seeds, stiring constantly, until brown. Or brown on ungreased cookie sheet in preheated 350° oven for 20 minutes, stirring occasionally. Grind toasted seed in a blender, or with a mortar and pestle. Add vinegar, lemon juice, sugar, soy sauce and MSG. Blend into smooth paste and combine with peanut oil. Store in covered jar.

Sprinkle chilled watercress and spinach with chives. Shake dressing well and pour on salad just before serving. Use only enough to coat leaves. Toss thoroughly.

Note: This sesame dressing is also excellent with Sesame Slaw.

SESAME SLAW

3 *cups finely shredded new*
   cabbage

2 *shredded young carrots*
½ *grated sweet onion*

Mix slaw ingredients with sesame dressing. Serve well chilled.

TOSSED GREEN SALAD
WITH ANCHOVY DRESSING

mixed salad greens
spinach leaves
1 red onion, sliced paper thin

Dressing:
¼ cup red wine vinegar
1 small can flat anchovy
    fillets, drained
1 small clove garlic
¼ tsp. each: oregano, sweet
    basil, thyme, tarragon
½ tsp. black pepper
½ cup olive oil

Combine tender leaves of various available salad greens. Add a few small tender spinach leaves, stems removed. Wash greens thoroughly in cold water. Drain and remove every drop of water from greens, even if it means blotting each leaf separately. Tear greens into manageable pieces. Store in refrigerator until ready to use. (An old clean pillow case makes a good storage bag.)

DRESSING: Pour a little vinegar into bowl of blender. Cut anchovy fillets into small pieces and add them a few at a time. Blend until smooth, scraping if necessary with rubber spatula and adding more vinegar from time to time. Repeat until all anchovies are blended. Add garlic clove, herbs, black pepper and balance of vinegar. Cover and blend into smooth paste. Remove contents of blender to bowl and slowly add olive oil, mixing well. Dressing will be quite thick. If you prefer, it can be thinned by adding additional oil and vinegar. It can be stored in a covered jar in the refrigerator for quite a long time.

To serve salad, combine thinly sliced red onion and salad greens. Toss with enough of the anchovy dressing to coat greens.

SWEET AND SOUR GARDEN SALAD

4 cucumbers
1 bunch red radishes
4 scallions

Dressing:
½ cup water
1 clove garlic
1 Tbsp. ginger root
3 shallots, chopped fine
2 tsps. powdered turmeric
1 tsp. salt
1 tsp. white pepper
¼ cup cider vinegar
¼ cup brown sugar

DRESSING: Combine water with garlic and ginger root, both squeezed through garlic press, shallots, powdered turmeric, salt and white pepper. Or blend all in blender until completely smooth. Simmer over low heat for 15 minutes, remove from heat and add vinegar and brown sugar. Stir and cool.

Peel and quarter cucumbers lengthwise. Scrape out and discard seeds. Slice cucumbers into diagonal ½-inch pieces. Clean and slice radishes paper thin. Cut scallions into ¼-inch diagonal slices, including green parts.

Place vegetables in a glass or pottery container and mix well with cooled dressing. Cover and keep in refrigerator for 4 hours or longer.

Excellent with grilled lamb, seafood or chicken dishes.
Serves 6.

INDIAN GARDEN SALAD

6 small cucumbers, peeled
  and chopped
2 large Bermuda onions,
  sliced paper thin
4 large beefsteak tomatoes,
  peeled and diced

1 Tbsp. salt
4 Tbsps. lime juice
1 tsp. prepared mustard
1 tsp. turmeric
½ pt. plain yoghurt

Sprinkle cucumbers, onions and tomatoes with salt. Let stand for 30 minutes. Drain excess juice.

Combine lime juice, mustard and turmeric with yoghurt. Pour over drained vegetables and chill until ready to use.

MINTED CUCUMBER SALAD WITH YOGHURT

6 *small cucumbers, peeled and sliced thin*
4 *scallions, with greens, chopped*
1 *bunch of red radishes, sliced thin*

2 *tsps. salt*
½ *clove garlic, pressed*
½ *tsp. pepper*
2 *Tbsps. fresh mint, chopped*
½ *pt. plain yoghurt*

Combine cucumbers, scallions and radishes. Season with salt. Let stand for 30 minutes. Press down and drain excess juice.

Combine garlic, pepper and chopped mint with yoghurt and blend thoroughly with drained vegetables.

Chill in a covered bowl.

AVOCADO ICE CREAM

1 *qt. vanilla ice cream*   1 *large ripe avocado*

Remove ice cream from freezer and allow to soften slightly.

Peel and mash avocado or force through sieve.

In a bowl mix avocado pulp thoroughly with ice cream.

Return mixture to carton and put in freezer for several hours before serving.

Note: This ice cream will have a delicate color and subtle flavor.

CHOCOLATE MOUSSE

8 oz. Mèniere chocolate
3 Tbsps. strong black coffee
½ cup plus 3 Tbsps. butter

6 eggs, separated
1½ cups whipping cream
1 Tbsp. superfine sugar

Melt chocolate in top of double boiler over gently simmering water. Add coffee and butter, stirring, as butter melts, to blend with chocolate.

Beat egg yolks until light and foamy. Stir into chocolate mixture. Remove from fire and cool.

Beat egg whites until stiff. Whip ½ cup cream with sugar until stiff. Fold beaten egg whites and whipped cream into cooled chocolate mixture.

Pour into a lightly buttered ring mold. Cover top with waxed or plastic paper and store in refrigerator until well set and thoroughly chilled.

Unmold onto serving dish. Serve with 1 cup stiffly whipped cream.

Serves 6 to 8.

Note: This is a rich chocolatey mousse which has always turned out successfully.

FRUIT MEDLEY WITH WHIPPED CREAM

fruits and berries
1 apricot sheet (available in
    specialty shops)
    or 6 tenderized apricots,
    cut into shreds

½ cup shredded moist
    coconut
1 cup whipping cream
1 Tbsp. sugar
2 oz. crème de Cacao

Note: The trick of this dessert is to combine as many different fruits and berries as you can. Use seasonal fresh fruit, mixed with frozen and canned.

Possibilities: Apricots, peaches, pineapple, tangerines, nectarines, melons, grapes, cherries, oranges, mangoes, papayas, strawberries, blueberries, raspberries, blackberries, plums. Add bananas at the last minute to prevent discoloration.

Peel, pit and slice fresh fruit. Seed and halve grapes. Cut melon into small balls. Stem and rinse berries. Thaw and drain frozen fruit and berries. Drain and slice canned fruit.

Place a colander in a bowl. Put fruit in colander and let it drain as it chills in refrigerator.

When ready to serve, transfer thoroughly drained fruit to serving bowl, and stir in slivers of sheet apricot or cut apricots and moist coconut shreds.

Whip chilled cream until it begins to thicken; add sugar, and continue whipping until stiff. Stir in crème de Cacao and fold whipped cream into drained fruit mixture.

RUM-CHESTNUT DESSERT

1 8-ounce jar marrons in
    syrup
4 oz. light rum

1 doz. lady fingers
½ pt. heavy cream

Pour rum into small bowl. Split lady fingers, dip them very lightly and quickly in rum and line a 1½-pint mold.

Whip cream until stiff. Pour marrons with syrup into bowl. crumble large pieces with a fork. Fold marrons into whipped cream and pile mixture into lined mold. Top with remaining lady fingers, pour balance of rum over all.

Cover with waxed paper or plastic wrap. Refrigerate overnight.

Will serve at least 6.

Some Specialty Shops

The following shops will fill mail orders:

Oriental foods (catalogues on request):

EASTERN TRADING COMPANY, 2801 Broadway, New York 25, N.Y.

JAPAN MART, 239 West 105 Street, New York 25, N.Y.

KATAGIRI, 224 East 59 Street, New York 22, N.Y.

ORIENTAL FOOD SHOP, 1302 Amsterdam Avenue 22, New York, N.Y.

Other special foods and spices:

MANGANARO FOODS, 488 Ninth Avenue, New York 18, N.Y. *(Italian)*

TRINACRIA IMPORTING COMPANY, 415 Third Avenue, New York 16, N.Y. *(spices, herbs, imported foods from many countries)*

PAPRIKAS WEISS, 1564 Second Avenue, New York 28, N.Y. *(Hungarian and Central European)*

JACK WITTKAMP, 320 50 Street, West New York, New Jersey *(Indonesian spices)*

M. KEHAYAN, 380 Third Avenue, New York 16, N.Y. *(Near and Middle East foods)*

MAISON GLASS, 52 East 58 Street, New York 22, N.Y. *(gourmet foods)*

LES ESCHALOTTES, 706 Lafayette Street, Paramus, New Jersey *(shallots)*

Index

Rum-chestnut dessert, 211
Russian-style lamb, 98

Saffron shrimp with coconut, bananas, almonds, 169-170
Sake, substitute for, 78
Salads:
  Indian garden, 208-209
  lentil, 205
  marinated asparagus, tomatoes, 203
  minted cucumber with yoghurt, 209
  sesame slaw, 206
  sweet and sour garden, 208
  three-bean, 204-205
  tossed green, anchovy dressing, 207
  watercress and spinach, sesame dressing, 206
Salami:
  miniature Holland, pickle chips, 46
  rolls with gherkins, 55
Salmon steaks with dill sauce, 151-152
Sardine dip, 41
Sasaties, 91
Saté ajam (Indonesian chicken), 131
Saté kambing (Indonesian lamb), 99
Sauces, see Dips and sauces
Sausages:
  with apples, 54
  Vienna, with hot mustard, 47
Savory brown rice with giblets, 191-192
Savory wild rice, 193
Scallops:
  with sardine dip, 41
  sesame, 42
  and shrimp with cashews, 172
  sweet and pungent, 173
Scampi, 166-167
Scandinavian shrimp, 35
Scrod fillets, 152
Seafood, see Fish and seafood; also under individual names
Seafood cocktail balls, sweet and sour sauce, 42-43

Sea squab, 152-153
Sesame:
  salad dressing, 206
  scallops, 42
  shrimp, 34
  shrimp with dill, 37
  slaw, 206
Sesame oil, 67
  substitute for, 68
Sesame seeds, how to toast, 98
Shad, 153-154
Shashlik, 92-93
  Caucasian, 93
  see also Kebabs; Shishkebab
Shellfish, see Fish and seafood; also under individual names
Shell steak au poivre, 74
Sherried chicken livers, 134
Sherried lamb and kidney kebabs, 96
Shirataki ("cellophane noodles"), 77
Shishkebab, 94
Shops filling mail orders, 213
Shoyu (soy sauce), 78
Shrimp:
  anchovy, 34-35
  Basque, 167-168
  with caviar dip, 35-36
  with cucumbers, curried pistachio butter, 170-171
  curried, with coconut, 168
  with dill and beer, 33
  hot mustard, 37
  jumbo, grilled in shell, 36
  -lobster surprise packages, 40
  and mussels Mediterranean, 171
  Oriental, 33
  preparation of, 33
  saffron, with bananas, nuts, 169-170
  and scallops with cashews, 172
  scampi, 166-167
  Scandinavian, 35
  sesame, 34
  sesame, with dill, 37
  skewered variations, 33-37
  à la Tahiti, 169
  tandoori, 166
  vodka, 34
Skewered shrimp variations, 33-37
Skewers, 18